SGT. RODNEY M. DAVIS
"The Making of a Hero"

John D. Hollis

Hugo House Publishers, Ltd.

ISBN: 978-1-936449-91-0
Library of Congress Control Number: 2017963697

Book Cover and Interior Design: Christa E. Kegl

Hugo House Publishers, Ltd.
Englewood, Colorado
Austin, Texas
WWW.HugoHousePublishers.com

To Andy, who happily goes along with all my
adventure schemes. Everyone should have a cheering section
and support system as enthusiastic as he is.

FORWARD

"Greater love has no one than this, that he lay down his life for his friends" - John 15:13

The story of the life and character of Medal of Honor recipient Sergeant Rodney M. Davis, U.S. Marine Corps, is a story needing to be told.

In our present day, the word hero is so liberally tossed about that it becomes difficult sometimes to give it value. The dictionary defines a hero as "a man of distinguished courage or ability, admired for his brave deeds and noble qualities." Given the opportunity to review this manuscript gave me the chance to experience the life of a true hero, his make-up, his character, in spite of his circumstance.

John Hollis has done an excellent job researching and bringing together the various aspects and influences on the life of Sgt. Rodney M. Davis.

In reading this story, I have come to know a brother-in-arms. Ironically, both Sgt. Davis and I returned home from Vietnam in mid-September 1967. Unfortunately, Sgt. Davis had given all he had so that the lives of those who were the recipients of his courageous sacrifice could be realized and their children and grandchildren could have life.

This book brings to fore a powerful message about a true American hero who happened to have been of African descent.

Regardless of how he may have been viewed by many, he had self-worth and, with it, he desired to bless others rather than himself. Sgt. Davis carried forth in the tradition of numerous others of African descent who have fought bravely and sacrificed much for this nation, which we call America and home, throughout its history. The strength and connectedness of the Davis family serves as an example of what we learn at home contributes so much to who we are. I thank the Davis family for their willingness to allow John Hollis to so ably share Sgt. Rodney M. Davis, U.S. Marine, with the world.

-    Charles M. Hood, Jr.
     MG (Ret) USVI

PREFACE

"A man distinguished by exceptional courage and nobility and strength" –
The first listed definition of a hero, according to Webster's on-line dictionary.

Too often today we think of heroes as little more than caricatures, buffed-up super-humans sporting long capes and flamboyant tights while blessed with incredible strength, speed and other remarkable attributes.

Comic book champions like Superman, Batman, Spiderman, Iron Man, Captain America, the Hulk and the like immediately come to mind.

The reality is that we walk among true heroes every day, even if we aren't always aware of having done so. They are regular men and women, ordinary folks who do extraordinary things when the time calls for it.

"Sometimes," President Barack Obama said during the moving White House ceremony on March 18, 2014 in which he righted a wrong by presenting the Medal of Honor to 24 recipients whose valor had been previously downplayed because of their race or ethnicity, "the heroes we seek are right in front of us."

Truer words could never have been spoken.

Sgt. Rodney M. Davis was taller than most at 6-foot-5, but he never leapt tall buildings with a single bound, nor was he more powerful than a locomotive or faster than a speeding bullet. He was a regular man with equally-as-real concerns and fears. What he did have in abundance, however, was enough courage and mental fortitude for 10 men.

Davis was just a young man in the prime of his life at the time of his death, meaning there's little doubt that he probably feared death as much as any of the rest of his fellow Marines during that vicious battle in the Que Son Valley on Sept. 6, 1967.

He had a wife and two small children and a large contingent of family back home, all of whom loved him dearly and eagerly awaited his return. Davis had much for which to live.

But it was likely that the fear of somehow letting down his new brothers in the U.S. Marine Corps scared Davis even more, so he did what he felt he needed to do without the slightest hesitation.

There's no shame in ever being frightened, as war is an especially scary business. Anybody who waxes poetic about it or in any way romanticizes it has clearly never seen its horrible face up close.

Yet, for better or worse, war has always been a fundamental part of our history, every bit as instrumental in mankind's development as any technological advances while reaching every distant corner of the globe and touching every generation.

War has always served as the stage to bring out the both the best and worst in men, often serving as a catalyst for change and an arena for valor. True courage is not the absence of fear during war, but the mastering of it.

What separates Sgt. Rodney M. Davis from so many other men is that he never let his fear get the best of him – he had always controlled it. Just as he had while growing up and consistently looking after his siblings amidst the oppression of Jim Crow.

He knew even while growing up that always doing right by those most in need of his help wasn't always going to be easy or without cost.

So it didn't make any difference to Davis that the men who were suddenly in harm's way when that grenade was tossed into their trench were all white men, at least one of whom he'd never even met before. It didn't matter to him at that critical moment that those who looked like him back home – his family included –

were fighting a war of a different kind back on American soil, one for their full equality as American citizens.

None of that mattered at that critical moment.

Those men suddenly in harm's way were all fellow Marines, and he considered them to be every bit his brothers as his siblings with whom he grew up in Macon. He grew up looking out for Gordon, Howard, Robert and Debra. He would do no less for his new brothers in the U.S. Marine Corps.

I would like to thank God for His many blessings and continued guidance in helping me finally bring to life the moving and heroic story of the late Sgt. Rodney M. Davis, a cherished family member and revered U.S. Marine who is Macon, Georgia's only Medal of Honor recipient.

Davis may be gone, but his legacy remains enduring.

His life – as much as his death – is proof that heroes are ordinary people who do extraordinary things at the most critical times, that greatness could hail from anywhere, regardless of age, pedigree or ethnicity.

His is a story that reverberates today, especially with young people of all colors who might question whether they matter, whether they, too, are capable of making such a difference and accomplishing something of similar significance. Time-honored attributes like honor, courage, duty, commitment, and sacrifice have always struck a powerful chord with all Americans.

It is also one that speaks in a time where racial tensions are again rising in America to the fact that we are all Americans first and foremost, that we share more things in common than we have that divide us.

This project wouldn't even have been possible without the unconditional love and support of my family, especially my wife Regina and Davis, our precocious young son. It was Regina, who is Sgt. Davis' niece, who initially piqued my curiosity after telling me of his scintillating story shortly after we first began dating.

Sgt. Davis' mother is no longer with us, but I had spoken at length with Ruth Amanda Davis a few years prior to her late August 2008 death about the prospect of someday doing a book project about her son. I'm pleased to say that "Granny" gave me her warmest blessings and encouragement. My hope now is to let the rest of the world know of Sgt. Rodney M. Davis and to make Granny and the entire Davis family proud.

That especially goes for Sgt. Davis' two daughters, Samantha and Nicky. Both women are very much proud, yet equally as sad when talking about their father. He gallantly died for his country, but that fact didn't always make up for the fact that Samantha and Nicky grew up without their dad. He wasn't there to see them mature from infant girls into the accomplished lawyer and banker they are today. He wasn't there to see them work their way through school, get married and then get on with their own lives complete with their own families.

To them, Rodney M. Davis was never the guy who is forever etched in U.S. military annals as one of the few African-Americans ever awarded the Medal of Honor. Not even the lauded war hero whose name graced a U.S. Navy warship.

He's always simply been Dad.

I would also like to especially thank Rodney Davis' four surviving siblings – Gordon Davis, Howard Davis, Robert Davis and Debra Ray – for their time, patience and willingness to consistently sit down and discuss with me an extremely sensitive subject that remains very painful to this day. I've come to know each of them very well and to love them all dearly after marrying into the Davis family in 2003, but I can only imagine how terribly difficult it would always be to revisit the loss of a beloved brother, especially at such a tender young age as 25.

And my sincerest gratitude also extends to Dr. Josephine Davis, Gordon Davis' wife and the sister-in-law of Sgt. Davis, for her help in recounting Rodney Davis' formative early years; and to John Reimers and Ted Blaine, my two very distinguished former English teachers at the Woodberry Forest School in Virginia, for their precious time and guidance in helping me better craft the story together.

I also wish to specifically recognize all the stalwart Marines of the 1/5 (First Battalion, Fifth Marine Regiment), but especially all those brave men of 2nd Platoon, Bravo Company who served with Sgt. Davis in Vietnam and were with him when he was killed on Sept. 6, 1967. It was hardly an easy decision for former platoon sergeant Ron Posey to initially agree to first meet with me in

Macon in late July 2009, and to discuss in great detail all that had happened that horrible day. Posey had never once prior discussed any part of his Vietnam experience with anyone since he left the country more than 40 years earlier. Not even with his late wife of nearly 40 years or any of his adult children. I will always feel honored beyond measure that he would make such a special exception for me because he so strongly believed this was a rousing story worth telling. And because he felt that he owed Rodney Davis at least that much for saving his life at the expense of his own.

I had driven down from Atlanta and met Posey in Macon on a bright Sunday morning, but it wasn't until well past 9 p.m. the night before did he finally muster the courage to call me and agree to sit and talk with me. He confessed that hadn't called me until the last possible minute because the memories were still that painful for him even after all those many years and he wasn't sure until that moment that he could actually go through with it. Posey respectfully asked that I come alone because he knew that he just couldn't face the entire Davis family at that time, and I soon understood why. Recounting the details of that awful day and how he survived to have a great life only because of Rodney Davis' sacrifice was emotional enough for him in just discussing it with me in the several hours we sat down in front of one another. I had tears running down my own eyes as well as he recalled the horrific story to me.

The same pretty much held true for Davis' former platoon leader, the late John Brackeen, and fellow Marines in Randy Leedom, Gary Petrous, Ben Drollinger, recently deceased former battalion commander, Peter L. Hilgartner, Rob MacNichol, Raymond Pistol and the many other brave Marines with whom I spoke. I can never thank these gentlemen enough for their patience as I consistently peppered them with repeated e-mails, phone calls and questions and more questions over a span of a few years. They are all very special men and I feel honored beyond measure to now call them close friends who are more like brothers to me. I will be forever indebted for the help given me by these true heroes and for all their tremendous service to our country.

I can't describe the tremendous joy and immense satisfaction it later brought me to see Posey, Leedom, Petrous and Drollinger and other 1/5 Vietnam veterans so warmly greeted in Macon by the entire Davis family and others during the activities leading up to and through the dedication of the Sgt. Rodney M. Davis Memorial Statue in November 2012.

It saddens me to report that Lt. Brackeen died in his native Texas from an aggressive form of cancer at the age of 67 on Jan. 24, 2010, just a few short days after we last spoke by phone. I also wish to sincerely thank his eldest grandson, Stevie Brackeen Turunc, and his widow, Gwen Brackeen, for all the valuable help they both graciously gave me in helping to piece together his life following his tenure in Vietnam and for their much-appreciated presence at the first of the two bi-annual cleanups at Sgt. Davis' gravesite in Macon in spring 2014.

Likewise, I wish to also note the death of Col. Hilgartner, who passed away in January 2015. Both Brackeen and Hilgartner were true patriots who provided critical help in the making of this book. Rest easy, Marines.

Repeated efforts to locate Lance Corporals Gregory Crandall and Lonnie Hinshaw were unsuccessful, so I relied on statements the two men made during Davis' Medal of Honor investigation for their take on the tragic events of Sept. 6, 1967. Additional comments from Hinshaw about what happened during Operation Swift were later found at the National Museum of the Marine Corps in Triangle, Va.

And we'd be remiss if we didn't give a shout out to the 1/5 Vietnam Veterans Association for all their support and critical help in putting me in touch with many of the veterans whom I interviewed. I can't say enough great things about treasurer, past president, former Marine platoon leader in Vietnam and noted author Nicholas Warr in particular for all of his efforts in helping to make this project a reality. Nick Warr was also very instrumental in putting me in touch with several of the Marines with whom I needed to speak, as well as with Lt. Col. Bill Cody, the retired and very gracious Marine and Vietnam veteran whose knowledge and expertise produced the Vietnam combat maps needed for this project.

Special thanks also goes to the Department of Defense and, in particular, the U.S. Marine Corps and the U.S. Navy for all their assistance, and to the first-class officers and crew of the USS Rodney M. Davis (FFG-60) for their time, graciousness and generosity during our family visit to the ship in late August 2009. My wife and I both became emotional as we prepared to come aboard, our hearts immediately tugged by the immaculate red carpet and the "Davis Family Boarding!" call that heralded our arrival just before the ship's skipper and senior officers all snapped to attention and saluted us.

It was an indelible moment I will always cherish.

My appreciation also extends to Congressman David Scott (D-Ga.) and his exemplary staff for their timely efforts in helping me cut through a maze of government red tape in quickly procuring Sgt. Davis' official military records. Having official documentation of all the key dates from his entire military career was a must for accuracy's sake.

I'd also like to acknowledge my family and those close friends and colleagues who listened so attentively on the many occasions I bounced the stirring story of Sgt. Rodney M. Davis by them for their opinions. My special gratitude goes to my two brothers, Andre and Rick Hollis, my brother-in-law, Howard Davis, Jr., and close friends Kevin Tydings, Stewart Verdery, Rich Gable, Holt Livesay, Jr., Steve Metzger, Steve DeShazo, Jeff Schultze, Mike Zitz, Paul Fogleman, Col. Jeff Stewart of the Army National Guard, Lt. Col. Steele McGonegal of the Army National Guard, Kevin "Doc" Johnson, Tom, Lorie and Cali Sullivan and the many, many others whose love, support and friendship helped keep me sane throughout the whole process.

I also wish to mention Curtis Bunn, a very accomplished author in his own right and my good friend and former Atlanta Journal-Constitution sports writing colleague, for his help, his time and his valued friendship over the years, not to mention his continued patience with me as I repeatedly picked his brain for professional advice.

Finally, let me say that Sgt. Rodney M. Davis was a man of extraordinary courage and unwavering principles, and to remember men like him and their sacrifices is to always honor them. I have tried to best illustrate how his unflinching devotion to his country, his family and his brothers-in-arms was a calling he faithfully answered starting a young age and a duty he felt compelled to uphold and how it was that his life, while cut well short, was well-lived.

I'm proud to say that, while writing this book, Sgt. Rodney M. Davis became a personal hero of sorts to me, and I only wish that I might have had the honor of having known him. I just hope that I have done him the justice he deserves in this work about his inspirational life and death.

- John D. Hollis

OFFICIAL CITATION

For conspicuous gallantry and intrepidity at the risk of his life above and beyond the call of duty while serving as the right guide of the Second Platoon, Company B, First Battalion, Fifth Marines, First Marine Division, in action against enemy forces in Quang Nam Province, Republic of Vietnam, on 6 September 1967. Elements of the Second Platoon were pinned down by a numerically superior force of attacking North Vietnamese Army Regulars. Remnants of the platoon were located in a trench line where Sergeant Davis was directing the fire of his men in an attempt to repel the enemy attack. Disregarding the enemy hand grenades and high volume of small arms and mortar fire, Sergeant Davis moved from man to man shouting words of encouragement to each of them while firing and throwing grenades at the onrushing enemy. When an enemy grenade landed in the trench in the midst of his men, Sergeant Davis, realizing the gravity of the situation, and in a final valiant act of complete self-sacrifice, instantly threw himself upon the grenade, absorbing with his own body the full and terrific force of the explosion. Through his extraordinary initiative and inspiring valor in the face of almost certain death, Sergeant Davis saved his comrades from injury and possible loss of life, enabled his platoon to hold its vital position and upheld the highest traditions of the Marine Corps and the United States Naval Service. He gallantly gave his life for his country.

Congressional Medal of Honor citation
Sgt. Rodney M. Davis (USMC)
Presented on March 26, 1969

CONTENTS

CHAPTER 1

THE MEDAL OF HONOR

It would be roughly 18 months following his death before his family learned that Sgt. Rodney M. Davis had been tapped to be posthumously awarded the Medal of Honor.

Established on July 12, 1862 by a joint resolution of Congress, the Medal of Honor is awarded in the name of Congress to a member of the armed services who distinguishes him or herself "conspicuously by gallantry and intrepidity at the risk of his/her life above and beyond the call of duty while engaged in an action against an enemy of the United States."

More than 40 million Americans have fought on behalf of their country since the nation's founding in 1776, but only fewer than 3,500 Medals of Honor have been awarded to our nation's bravest soldiers, sailors, airmen, marines and coast guardsmen, according to the Mt. Pleasant, South Carolina-based Congressional Medal of Honor Society.

The earliest actions for which the Medal was awarded took place before the official start of the Civil War, according to the Medal of Honor society. Bernard J.D. Irwin, an assistant surgeon in the Army, performed the first action deserving of the Medal of Honor when he voluntarily led a command of troops to relieve a surrounded detachment of the Seventh Infantry engaged against hostile Apache Indians from February 13-14, 1861. Irwin, however, was not awarded the Medal until more than 30 years later in 1894.

On March 25, 1863, Army Private Jacob Parrott became the first of a group of six men to actually be awarded the Medal of Honor for their heroism during a mission deep within enemy territory in Georgia to destroy Confederate supply lines in April 1862.

As of the start of the summer of 2017, only 88 had been awarded to African-American Marines, servicemen, according to the Medal of Honor Society. Sergeant William Harvey Carney, a former slave, is credited as the first African-American recipient for the award after performing heroically on July 18, 1863 with the famed, all-black 54th Massachusetts Volunteer Infantry during an assault on Confederate-held Fort Wagner in South Carolina. The battle was immortalized in the 1989 Academy Award-winning movie "Glory" that starred Denzel Washington, Morgan Freeman and Matthew Broderick.

Carney, who didn't receive the Medal of Honor until nearly 37 years later, had been shot in the face, shoulders, arms, and legs, but refused to let the American flag touch the ground.

Because of the lengthy delay in recognizing Carney's actions, Robert Blake, a Union sailor and a former slave, became the first African-American to actually receive the Medal of Honor when he was honored on April 16, 1864 for his heroism in the face of withering Confederate fire while serving aboard the gunboat USS Marblehead a few months earlier.

Robert Augustus Sweeney, also a sailor in the U.S. Navy, is one of just 19 Americans and the only African-American to have twice been awarded the Medal of Honor.

Corporal John Mackie became the first of 299 Marines to have received the medal when he was so honored in 1862 for valor in a Civil War battle in Richmond.

Mary Edwards Walkers, a Civil War surgeon, is the only female Medal of Honor recipient. Her medal was initially rescinded in 1917 along with many other non-combat awards, but was later restored by President Jimmy Carter in 1977.

There have been 59 Hispanic-Americans, 33 Asian-Americans and 32 Native Americans to have been honored with the medal, according to the Medal of Honor Society.

Racism throughout the armed forces played a key role in the shockingly low number of African-Americans so honored, according to a study first commissioned by the Army in 1993 to investigate racial discrimination in the awarding of medals.

At the time, no Medals of Honor had been awarded to any black soldiers who had served in World War II. After an exhaustive review of files, the study recommended that several African-American Distinguished Service Cross recipients be upgraded to the Medal of Honor.

President Bill Clinton would subsequently belatedly award the medal to seven African-American World War II veterans on January 13, 1997. With the passing of Vernon Baker in July 2010, all of the recipients have now died.

Clinton awarded 21 more new medals in 2000 following a similar study of Asian-Americans that had been conducted in 1998. Medals were awarded to 20 members of the 442nd Regimental Combat Team, whose members included Daniel Inouye, the late U.S. Senator from Hawaii. In 2005, President George W. Bush awarded the Medal of Honor to Tibor Rubin. The Jewish Korean War veteran and Holocaust survivor was believed to have been deliberately overlooked because of his religion.

President Barack Obama followed suit and did likewise on March 18, 2014, correcting a historical act of discrimination when he awarded the Medal of Honor to 24 veterans deemed by a 12-year Pentagon review to have been originally passed over for the nation's highest military honor because of their racial or ethnic backgrounds. Just three of the 24 men whose original citations were upgraded were still alive to be feted at the White House.

But better they were honored late than never at all.

"This ceremony reminds us of one of the enduring qualities that make America great – that make us exceptional," Obama said during the remarkable televised ceremony from the White

House's East Room. "No nation is perfect, but here in America, we confront our imperfections and face a sometimes painful past, including the truth that some of these soldiers fought and died for a country that did not always see them as equal.

"So with each generation, we keep on striving to live up to our ideals of freedom and equality, and to recognize the dignity and patriotism of every person, no matter who they are, what they look like or how they pray."

The soldiers accounted for the largest single group of Medal of Honor recipients since World War II. The president made sure to read the citations for all 24 men, with proud family members accepting the honor on behalf of their deceased relatives.

"Every one is a story of bravery that deserves to be told," Obama said.

Army Sgt. First Class Melvin Morris, an African-American from Port St. John, Fla., served two tours of duty in Vietnam and was among the U.S. Army's first Special Forces warriors better known as the Green Berets. He was among the large group of Medal of Honor recipients to be hailed by the president and stands as the most recent living African-American to be so recognized.

The accolade was long overdue, but wasn't the last racially-motivated Medal of Honor omission to be corrected.

In late August 2014, then-Secretary of Defense Chuck Hagel formally recommended that the Medal of Honor be posthumously awarded to Private Henry Johnson, an African-American World War I soldier who saved a comrade while fighting off a German attack. Johnson was among the two soldiers from World War I who were posthumously presented the Medal of Honor by President Obama on June 2, 2015. Sgt. William Shemin, a soldier of Jewish descent, was also feted for his bravery with the nation's highest award for valor.

A former railroad porter from Albany, N.Y., Johnson was a private serving with the U.S. Army's all-black 369th Infantry Regiment on May 15, 1918 when he ignored his own injuries to single-handedly fight off the attack and prevent the Germans from carrying off his wounded comrade.

For his actions, Johnson became one of the first Americans to be awarded the French Croix de Guerre avec Palme, France's highest award for valor.

It is believed that racism was the reason why Johnson was not honored at the time with the Medal of Honor. He returned home following the end of World War II, but struggled with alcoholism as he mended from his wounds. Johnson was estranged from his family and destitute upon his death at age 32 in 1929 at an Illinois veterans hospital. He was buried at Arlington National Cemetery.

President Obama and Congress pledged to correct similar injustices in the future.

While war is ugly and tragic with no real winners, no one questions that the many valiant individuals such as Sgt. Rodney M. Davis and the many others who have been awarded the Medal of Honor have displayed outstanding courage, valor and a willingness to make the ultimate sacrifice on behalf of their country when called to battle.

Theirs is an exclusive club few are privileged to join, no matter their rank or pedigree. General Douglas McArthur, a World War II icon, once said he'd sell his soul for a Medal of Honor. Legend has it that Gen. George Custer was so jealous of the two Medals of Honor awarded to his brother, Thomas, during the Civil War that the two men got into a fight when Thomas wore his medals to a social event.

Harry Truman once said he'd rather have the Medal of Honor than be president.

The medal has long been held in the highest regard, but especially by those who have worn the uniform and know from first-hand experience the bravery behind it. General Dwight D. Eisenhower was the architect of the Allied invasion of Europe that began with the landing at Normandy on June 6, 1944 that paved the way for the fall of the Third Reich, but he balked when talk of his being awarded the Medal of Honor later came up. The future president of the United States was adamant in declining, saying that such hallowed recognition should only go to men whose lives were directly in danger as a result of being in combat.

The award is so revered that tradition to this day dictates that all living Medal of Honor recipients are to be immediately saluted by all other military members, including superior officers ranging from generals and admirals and even all the way up to our nation's commander-in-chief, the president of the United States. In doing so, they are not only saluting the soldier, but also showing their tremendous respect for the award and the extraordinary act of heroism behind it.

Unlike many awards and decorations (both military and civilian) established and presented over the decades, the standards for the Medal of Honor have stiffened considerably over time – particularly since World War I – to the point that it is now near impossible to go "above and beyond the call of duty" and survive the action for which a service member might receive the award.

Consequently, there have been many extraordinarily brave American soldiers whose deeds – though recognized with other very prestigious citations and perhaps perceived by many others to even be worthy of the Medal of Honor – either did not meet the Medal's demanding criteria or there simply were not enough surviving witnesses of the specific action to recommend it. Additionally, the nature of combat has changed in the modern, more technologically-sophisticated era, meaning there are considerably fewer opportunities for the kind of valor deemed worthy of the Medal.

Army Staff Sgt. Salvatore Giunta, 25, became the first living recipient to be awarded the Medal since the Vietnam War when President Obama honored him on November 17, 2010 for his actions in Afghanistan three years earlier. The president later similarly honored Army staff sergeant Leroy Petry on July 15, 2011 and Marine Corporal Dakota Meyer on Sept. 15, 2011 for their heroism in Afghanistan. Meyer became the first living Marine recipient of the Medal of Honor in 41 years. There were no living medal recipients from the conflict in Iraq.

U.S. Navy SEAL Edward C. Beyers became the most recent recipient from the conflict in either Iraq or Afghanistan when President Obama awarded him the medal on Feb. 29, 2016 for gallantry in Afghanistan a little more than three years earlier.

An earlier recipient, U.S. Marine Lance Corporal William Kyle Carpenter White, miraculously survived after lunging on a

Taliban grenade in Afghanistan to save a fellow Marine in 2010, but suffered catastrophic injuries. Now a full-time student at the University of South Carolina who recovered enough from his life-threatening injuries to parachute in before running the 39th Annual Marine Corps Marathon in October 2014, Carpenter is among the 72 living recipients as of June 2017, according to the Medal of Honor Society.

Three recipients previous to Giunta from the war in Afghanistan, four from the Iraq war and two others from the Somalia campaign in 1993 had all been killed in action, according to that organization's website.

Like all the other presidents before him, Obama has consistently made sure to lavish great praise on all the most recent honorees, as well as all their predecessors.

"They are the very best part of us," the president said during the moving tribute to Giunta, according to a transcript released by the White House. "They are our friends, our family, our neighbours, our classmates, our co-workers. They are why our banner still waves, our founding principles still shine, and our country – the United States of America – still stands as a force for good all over the world."

The decision to endorse Davis for the nation's highest military award had been borne in the weeks immediately following his death, starting officially at the behest of Brackeen before working all the way up the chain of command for final approval. Unofficially, it was Leedom, then a lance corporal, and the several other enlisted men who fought alongside Davis that unforgettable day who were so inspired by what they saw that they helped to initially jumpstart the effort. Four witnesses are required for even consideration for the award.

Sgt. Rodney M. Davis (photo courtesy of the U.S. Marine Corps)

Their consistent testimony to the day's events were key to Davis' recognition.

Vice-President Spiro T. Agnew presents the Medal of Honor to the family of Sgt. Rodney M. Davis at the White House on March 26, 1969. (photo courtesy of the White House)

"On 6 September 1967, we were engaged with the enemy when they out-flanked us all the sides," Crandall testified during the subsequent Medal of Honor investigation, according to Pentagon records. "We pulled back and regrouped in a trench surrounding a bomb crater. There were about seven people in a 20-foot area in this trench when the enemy started their advance. We were putting out a base of fire when we started to receive incoming grenades ... Sgt. Davis saw the danger to myself and the rest of the Marines in the area. He threw himself intentionally on this grenade and sacrificed his life to save the men in the trench. I believe he should receive this award for service above and beyond the call of duty. Myself, my platoon commander and Lance Corporal Hinshaw are alive today because of Sgt. Davis' act of heroism."

Hinshaw agreed, saying "On 6 September 1967, I witnessed the actions of Sergeant Davis while on Operation Swift. My platoon was pinned down around a bomb crater when the NVA started attacking our position with heavy automatic fire. Sgt. Davis effectively directed his men's fire to stave off the attacking enemy. The enemy again assaulted our position, this time getting within hand grenade range. I believe there were about four [grenades] thrown at us, three of them landed outside the trench, the other one hit me in the leg and fell into the trench as I rolled out of the trench.

"At this time, Sergeant Davis saw the hand grenade and the danger to the men left in the trench. Sergeant Davis, seeing the grenade, dropped down on it, using his body to protect the other men in the trench from the explosion. I feel that he knew what he was doing and gave his life to save the five lives of his fellow Marines. I am alive today due to his actions."

Posey's official account of the day's dramatic events echoed that of the others.

"On 6 September 1967, we were pinned down and trapped in a bomb crater," he said. "The enemy had maneuvered close enough to throw hand grenades into our positions. Sgt. Davis was efficiently leading the men near his position and directing their fire when a series of hand grenades was thrown by the enemy. One of the grenades fell into the trench in which Sgt. Davis and six other Marines had their positions. He realized the danger to his fellow Marines and sacrificed his life to save theirs. I know he knew the grenade was there and that he intentionally fell on top of it to save the lives of other Marines. Myself and the other Marines are the only survivors of this action and we owe our lives to his sacrifice."

A thorough official investigation ensued and found that Davis had *"intentionally and with forethought, sacrificed his own life in one final act of selfless heroism to save the lives of his comrades,"* according to Pentagon records. The inquiry concluded that if Davis *"had not chosen to fall on the grenade, undoubtedly at least three of his comrades would have lost their lives or would have been seriously wounded."*

In a dispatch to Secretary of the Navy John Chafee, Gen. Robert E. Cushman, the Commanding General of the Third Marine Amphibious Force, supported the comprehensive investigation's results, lauding Davis for *"deliberately and intentionally"* smothering the grenade with his own body.

The Nov. 18, 1967 letter added that, *"Although the witnesses do not clearly indicate that Sergeant Davis had an avenue of escape, it appears, that in all probability, he could have at least evaded the full impact of the grenade without evidencing any cowardice whatsoever on his part."*

Army General William C. Westmoreland, the commander of all U.S. forces in Vietnam, formally approved the recommendation to posthumously award Davis the Medal of Honor in a memo dated Jan. 4, 1968. President Lyndon B. Johnson would ultimately sign off on the recommendation as well, cementing Davis' lofty status as one of the scant few African-Americans ever awarded the Medal of Honor.

Twenty of those troops – including five African-American Marines - were honored for actions occurring during the Vietnam War.

It was in early March 1969 that Judy Davis was sitting in a dentist chair in Macon when word reached her that the family had a Marine Corps visitor. She quickly became very excited, thinking somehow that there had been a big mistake of some kind and that the dress blue-clad Marine had come to tell her that that Rodney Davis was actually still alive.

The heartbroken widow later cried with great disappointment after learning that the purpose of his visit was "only" to tell her that her late husband was being posthumously awarded the Medal of Honor for his heroic actions in Vietnam.

"I was young," Judy Davis admitted during a 1987 interview with the Macon Courant. "I didn't know what that meant at the time."

Richard M. Nixon had since become the U.S. president by the time the Marine Corps flew the entire Davis family to Washington, D.C. to proudly accept the Medal of Honor at the White House on their late loved one's behalf during an 11:30 a.m. ceremony on March 26, 1969. Mayor Ronnie Thompson accompanied the family to the nation's capital to honor one of Macon's own.

Vice President Spiro T. Agnew formally presented the award to the family in the Executive Office Building, along with an official citation that lauded Davis' *"extraordinary initiative and inspiring valor in the face of almost certain death."*

"Mere words are inadequate to express the gratitude of this country," Agnew told a proud, but still grieving Davis family, according to media accounts the following day by both the New York Times and United Press International (UPI), *"but let it be said that his actions on behalf of his country, his selfless conduct and courage will stand as an example for young men for years to come and for generations not yet born."*

His family members had only first learned of the specific details behind Sgt. Rodney M. Davis' death while en route to Washington, D.C.

Davis' other medals and decorations included the Purple Heart, the Good Conduct Medal, the National Defense Service Medal, the Armed Forces Expeditionary Medal, the Vietnam Service Medal, the Military Merit Medal, the Gallantry Cross with Palm and the Republic of Vietnam Campaign Medal.

CHAPTER 2

MOVING FORWARD

The noted author and historian, the late Stephen E. Ambrose, once wrote that one day's trial by battle reveals more of the essential nature of people than any generation of peace.

I have always preferred to also think that's true, that we easily learn more about people during their darkest hours and most challenging times than when everything around them is going smoothly. Adversity, I've long held, exposes character rather than builds it.

So that's why I've been brimming with optimism about the future of race relations in our country and about humanity in general after first hearing of the inspiring story of Sgt. Rodney M. Davis' life and his death.

Rodney M. Davis represented the best humanity had to offer. Like the rest of us, he was far from perfect. But it's safe to say the world would be a much better place if there were more folks like him who adhered to the ideals for which they stood.

And for which he died.

Davis had been living an exemplary life of honor, courage and commitment long before receiving a Marine Corps emblem to signify his embodiment of such traits. Looking after those who needed help in fending for themselves had been his life's calling, starting with his four siblings as they grew up under the oppression of Jim Crow in Macon, Georgia. He would do no less for his new brothers in the U.S. Marine Corps.

My wife and I had just begun dating when she first told me that her uncle had been posthumously awarded the Medal of Honor in the Vietnam War after jumping atop an enemy grenade to save the lives of several of his fellow Marines. That immediately commanded the attention of an avid American history buff like myself, not to mention my utmost respect and almost giddy admiration of anybody who could have been so incredibly brave.

But the already riveting story just got better still the deeper I dug into it. It was only later in doing my own research and countless interviews with other Marines there that day did I discover that the five men whose lives were spared when Sgt. Davis sacrificed his own by jumping on the grenade all just happened to be white.

Not even members of the Davis family had been aware of this dynamic twist to the story. They had just naturally assumed for the last several decades that at least some of the men closest to Sgt. Rodney M. Davis at the time of his death in combat had been African-American as well. It was hardly an unreasonable assumption, given the controversial charges over the disproportionate number of young black men being forced into duty along Vietnam's dangerous front lines in the war's early years.

The revelation rocked me to the core because I was very much aware of how the polarizing issue of black and white had very much threatened to rip the country asunder in 1967, as more than 150 American cities endured very costly and destructive race riots during that summer. And because I knew well of just how deeply the issue of race had always adversely affected the daily lives of Davis and his siblings as they grew up under Jim Crow's unforgiving boot in Macon, Georgia.

In an unfortunate sign of the times in Macon and many other parts of America, Davis was deemed good enough to be sent to a distant land thousands of miles away to fight and die for his beloved country alongside equally-as-brave white Marines, yet not worthy of even eating alongside those same comrades-in-arms in restaurants back in his own hometown. He was too often forced to defend himself and those he cared about in Macon just as he was in Vietnam.

Yet his inspiring story is an All-American tale of courage and sacrifice that resonates with people of all colors and creed. Davis wasn't flawless by any means, but he looked to always stay true to his convictions of doing right by others and always helping those in need.

Ultimately at the expense of his own life.

His actions throughout his life and his death in Vietnam embodied the same time-honored values long held so dear by the U.S. Marine Corps.

Honor, Courage, and Commitment.

I have 16 years of daily newspaper experience, almost all as a sportswriter, and have run the gamut of fascinating stories and famous folks I've met along the way. I've covered the NFL, the Super Bowl, the Olympics, the NBA, five NCAA college basketball Final Fours, the College Baseball World Series and major college football and basketball in both the SEC and ACC among other things. Never, however, have I come across a more powerful and compelling tale as that of Sgt. Rodney M. Davis.

The fact that it was a true story and centered around my own father-in-law's brother made it all that much more enticing to me.

That's because it would have been so very easy – and perhaps somewhat even understandable to some degree - for Davis to have been bitter about the shoddy treatment that he, his family members and other African-Americans had endured in Macon and throughout many other parts of the nation. Given the turbulent times and venomous racial climate in his own hometown and throughout many parts of the U.S. at the time, some like myself who have never served might have even grasped at some level if perhaps Davis had hesitated ever so slightly or perhaps did nothing at all at the critical moment rather than martyr himself to spare the lives of five white Marines he barely knew, if at all.

That Davis sacrificed his own life without hesitation to spare the lives of several of his fellow Marines who happened to be white speaks volumes about the man, his principles and his unflinching courage even in the face of certain death.

Davis dearly loved America, no matter its faults.

It didn't matter in the least to him on Sept. 6, 1967 that the five men whose lives were suddenly in danger from the enemy grenade suddenly at their feet happened to all be white. They were all his brothers in the U.S. Marine Corps, and he'd been raised to always take care of his own.

Likewise, necessity assured that the men with whom Davis directly served didn't see color either, as everybody along the front lines in the Que Son Valley in September 1967 was entirely dependent on one another for their very survival. No matter their race, creed or pedigree.

The irony in it all is almost too rich to ignore.

Too many previously close-minded Americans had to first be shipped off thousands of miles away to Southeast Asia and then be shot at in what was the closest thing to hell on earth at the time to experience what America is supposed to have been about all along. Namely the kind of brotherhood where a man's color mattered less than his character and ability.

The Vietnam War was our nation's first fully integrated one, often placing many whites and African-Americans together in close proximity for long periods for the first time. But I take great pleasure in noting that race didn't appear to be an issue in any way for the many brave, young Marines of Bravo Company, First Battalion, Fifth Regiment, First Marine Division who fought in Operation Swift in September 1967.

They were brothers in every sense, their bond forever forged by the shared blood, sweat and tears in the nastiest jungles and soggiest rice paddies of the Que Son Valley.

If these young men from parts all over could endure the most trying of combat conditions while thousands of miles away from home and still put aside their own inherent prejudices, stereotypes and cultural differences all for the greater good, then there's no reason to believe we can't all do likewise if we so put our minds to it.

Many men speak of attaining such lofty goals, but Sgt. Rodney M. Davis had lived his entire life doing as much. Though heartbroken by his loss, his family and friends were hardly surprised to have heard that he died in the same heroic manner in which he'd lived.

It's often been said that heroes are the sinews of any great nation, inspiring others following behind to greatness as well. We could use more such men today.

For the many who bravely served, the Vietnam War likely ranks as among the most defining events in their lives. As you might imagine, it was hardly an easy thing for the many veterans with whom I spoke for this project to again dredge up the many difficult memories and feelings of deep loss that come from seeing so many close friends horribly cut down in the prime of their lives. However, they all did so with tremendous grace and with great pride in what they accomplished for their country.

And for one another.

However, I quickly discovered that the large passage of time was going to be the biggest obstacle to be overcome in trying to accurately writing a book largely based on first-hand accounts. Memories understandably fade as folks get older, meaning recollections of the same events can vary somewhat from person to person. Specific conversations have been recalled as best as possible, but the essence of each of those very telling dialogues remains accurate.

But, by using as many resources available to me, and constantly checking and re-checking with all my sources, I think I have come up with as close to an accurate sequence of events as is possible after 50 years.

I figured I owed Sgt. Rodney M. Davis at least that much for his gallant service and tremendous sacrifice on the behalf of all the rest of us.

CHAPTER 3

THE BULLY IN THE MAKING

Often called "The Heart of Georgia" because of its location in the central part of the state, Macon lies on the site of the Ocmulgee Old Fields, which had originally been home to the Creek Indians and their predecessors as long as 1,200 years before the first Europeans arrived.

The city boasts one of Georgia's three fall lines, joining both Augusta and Columbus. The fall line is where hilly lands of the Piedmont plateau meet the flat terrain of the coastal plain. As such, Macon boasts a varied landscape, with rolling hills in the north and flat plains in the southern section. The fall line is responsible for rivers in the area always declining rapidly toward sea level, making Macon an ideal location for textile mills in the past.

Prior to its establishment as a city, Macon was the site of Fort Benjamin Hawkins. After the Creeks had ceded their lands east of the Ocmulgee River, President Thomas Jefferson ordered the fort built in 1806 on the river's fall line to protect the new frontier. The post later became a major military distribution point during the War of 1812 and the subsequent Creek War of 1813, but was later essentially discarded before eventually burning to the ground a few years later.

A year after the establishment of Bibb County in 1822, the city was originally chartered by settlers from North Carolina and officially named Macon in honor of North Carolina statesman Nathaniel Macon, a staunch slavery and states' rights advocate.

Thanks to its fortuitous location on the Ocmulgee River, Macon soon began to thrive economically, with cotton serving as the city's main staple. Cotton boats, stage coaches and a railroad built in 1843 soon transformed the city into a major transportation hub while bringing unprecedented prosperity.

Much like the South as a whole, however, slavery was the backbone of Macon's economic vitality. But the resistance of African-Americans in the area to their continued oppression made international news in 1848 when Macon natives, William and Ellen Craft, fled to Philadelphia in a daring bid for freedom.

Ellen Craft, the daughter of an African-American woman and her white master, had skin light enough to allow her to pass for white. To avoid detection, she cut her hair short and wore a top hat as to better disguise herself as an ailing white gentleman planter. With her husband masquerading as his master's slave, the couple traveled openly by carriage, passenger train and steamship to the North rather than use the secretive and more dangerous routes of the Underground Railroad.

The Crafts eventually settled in Boston, where they began taking part in anti-slavery lectures throughout New England. Fearful of being recaptured and sent back into slavery, the Crafts moved to England before eventually returning to Georgia in 1870.

During the Civil War, Macon served as the official arsenal for the Confederacy, with Camp Oglethorpe housing captured Union officers and enlisted men before its closing in 1864. Macon City Hall briefly served as Georgia's capital following General William Tecumseh Sherman's invasion of Atlanta and destructive march to the sea that same year.

Macon was spared a similar fate, and its quaint downtown still showcases an array of beautiful antebellum houses that date back to those days. Today, Macon boasts more listings on the National Register of Historic Places than any other city in the state.

Yet racial inequities in Macon also survived following the end of the war, again surfacing during the years of Reconstruction. Old habits die hard in Georgia.

But music had long been the one love both Macon's black and white citizens had shared, and it was that mutual passion that has since helped the city in crossing the racial divide that has been segregation's legacy and forming initial bridges of trust. The kazoo was invented in Macon during the 1840s, while the city would later serve as the birthplace or hometown to such distinguished musical talents as The Allman Brothers Band, Little Richard, Otis Redding, Young Jeezy and many others.

The city's strong musical heritage eventually led to the construction of the Georgia Music Hall of Fame in Macon, showcasing musicians from around the state for their contributions in Georgia's distinguished music history.

But there was still a long ways to go in improving things when Ruth and Gordon N. Davis, Sr. welcomed the birth of their second son, Rodney Maxwell Davis, on April 7, 1942. Named "Rodney" as his mother's choice of a "romantic name" and "Maxwell" after the husband of Gordon's oldest sister, he was a welcomed second addition to the young family.

Over the course of his first years, Rodney quickly became the undisputed king of the Davis household, even sleeping with his mom on many occasions while his dad was away completing his service in the Navy. His brother Gordon was his senior by roughly 18 months, but Rodney had always been the much more assertive of the two, readily taking charge in their father's absence.

Despite the "reversal of the birth order" as family members often liked to joke, the two brothers had always been extremely close.

"Almost like twins," said their sister Debra.

She'd get no argument from Charlie Bell, the cousin who grew up in the Davis family home along with her own four siblings. The girls had nowhere to go following the death of their own parents, so Ruth Amanda Gordon wasted no time in extending them a place a stay alongside her own family.

It wasn't exactly easy packing as many as 10 young kids and two adults all under the same roof and properly seeing after them all during the late 1940s and early 1950s, but family meant everything to the Davis matriarch and she wasn't about to see her young nieces left unattended and possibly split up in an unforgiving foster care system.

Family did for family.

Bell, who, at 12, was the oldest of the five girls, did her part around the house by handling all the cooking – breakfast, lunch and dinner – for everybody while also making sure to do her sisters' hair each morning. Forced to grow up quickly by difficult life circumstances beyond her control, she often watched over the cadre of children in the house while Ruth Amanda Davis and her husband were out.

That meant consistently feeding them, changing diapers, looking after them and even serving as a willing playmate when needed. Her duties seemed endless at times.

But Bell quickly came to have a special affinity for Rodney.

"Rodney was a real special one in my book," says Bell, now retired and living in Macon. "He was real, real sweet and always so down-to-earth. He didn't favor anybody. He just loved everybody."

As you can imagine in a house with so many young children running around, there was a certain level of chaos at times, although Bell says that was more the exception than the norm. Gordon Davis, Sr. and his wife were adamant about everybody always adhering to their specific instructions when living under their roof.

"They had very strict rules," she recalled.

Chief among them was their insistence that each of the kids living under their roof always look out for one another. They would always be family, no matter whatever petty differences that may have come up between them. And that meant acting like family at all times and consistently watching one another's backs.

These basic tenets were non-negotiable, and Gordon and Ruth Amanda Davis made certain all of the children always knew what was expected of them. They were to promptly get up early each day for school, make up their beds, clean their rooms, take their baths and sit down at the table and eat their breakfasts before Ruth Amanda Davis drove them to school. The Davis boys attended the nearby private Catholic school in St. Peter Claver, while their cousins enrolled at the local public school.

But the children always found time to have fun with one another and their friends at the end of each day. Rodney and

Gordon lived for the outdoors, playing outside sports such as football, baseball, volleyball and basketball as much as their friends and parents would indulge them. Rodney stayed especially busy and constantly on the go, recalled Florie "Cherry" Fultes, a childhood friend of the Davis children who is now a retired civilian Air Force employee.

"If somebody was playing, [Rodney] was going to be there playing, too," she said. "He had all that energy."

Always quick with a joke and ready to have fun, Rodney often came up with innovative ways to keep everybody amused during the few times the children would actually grow weary of the same sports and outdoor activities they liked so much, Bell said.

But it was something special about Rodney that endeared him to Bell. Anybody can recite a joke, but delivering it at that special time when people were most in need a good laugh had long been Rodney's special gift, Bell said.

He always seemed to know just what to say or do at just the right occasion.

Bell recalled one specific hazy, summer afternoon in which all the kids were hot, tired and really not in the mood to play any more sports. Heading inside to squander the rest of the day from a comfortable position on the cushy couch to play mindless video games wasn't an option back in those days. Most kids back in that time period had been compelled by their parents and had no choice but to go out and exercise. So it was for the Davis kids, whose primary concerns were to just make sure they didn't stray too far from home and to always be home before dark.

Normally, recruiting other kids to play wasn't ever a problem of any kind, but spirits were lagging in the face of the blistering summer heat on this one particular late afternoon. Rodney Davis could sense as much and suddenly began laughing aloud.

"What's so funny?" one of the neighborhood kids then asked him.

Rodney coolly pretended that he hadn't heard the initial question and continued laughing aloud, piquing his friends' growing curiosity even further.

"What is so funny?" they asked again.

It was then that Rodney casually surveyed their faces, and knew that he had their complete and undivided attention.

"Ya'll want to see something funny?" he finally responded.

"Sure!" they shot back almost in unison.

Without as much as another word, Rodney quickly ran into the house, emerging just moments later with something in his hand. Unsure as to what was happening, the rest of the kids sat there quietly watching as Rodney uncapped the bottle of hot sauce he had with him and began making his way over to the dog nearby.

After pouring some of the hot sauce on his hand, he proceeded to bend down and rub it against the dog's back legs and buttocks area.

The stunned animal immediately took off in a fit, darting around the yard while simultaneously barking and wiping himself in the cool grass in the search of relief.

The kids erupted into laughter as Rodney had broken the ice with a timely boost of much-needed enthusiasm. The "victim" in this prank was just fine, too, as Rodney loved dogs and would never have intentionally hurt one. He quickly made sure to clean the dog off and rid him entirely of the uncomfortable effects of the hot sauce.

But young Rodney could immediately sense the buoyed spirits among his friends and finally allowed himself a wide grin.

"Now, c'mon, let's go play!" he said.

****

Gordon Davis, Sr. spent nearly two years in the U.S. Navy, getting out in February 1946 as a Petty Officer 3rd Class. He immediately returned home following the completing of his tour of duty just a few months following the end of World War II, but his transition home didn't go as smoothly as he would have liked. Rodney in particular grappled with the sudden change in his own status around the household.

No longer was he the undisputed man of the house or the one sleeping in bed next to his dear mother.

"Who is this man?" Rodney would sometimes bark aloud about his father. "When is this guy finally leaving our house?"

"Now, Rodney, be respectful because that's your father," Ruth Amanda Davis would caution her son.

"I don't know this man," Rodney would sometimes shoot back in return.

"But you will," his wise mother countered. "He's your father."

But Ruth and Gordon Davis were always understanding of the confusion of sorts that young Rodney initially experienced upon his father's return and remained patient as he began establishing those critical lifelong bonds with his father and came to terms with his own new role in the house. His parents knew it would take some time for father and son to get know one another again after being apart for so long on a daily basis. Fortunately, it didn't take that long.

Rodney and Gordon soon came to know, love and respect their father well, with each emulating him the best they could. Gordon Davis, Sr. was the unquestioned authority in the house and he took it upon himself to teach his impressionable young sons how to be good men who had a strong sense of civic duty and personal responsibility.

And that long process began with how they would treat one another.

Always alert and very inquisitive, Rodney lived a normal active childhood for which many southern boys are often renowned. That included lots of hunting, fishing, swimming and other plied skills from his many hours playing in the backyard.

It helped considerably that the brothers never had to go far when looking for something fun to do. The neighborhood was almost always bustling with activity from the many children of roughly the same age also living in the area.

Located just a few minutes' walk from the Davis home, the nearby Ocmulgee River was among the most popular spots for the Davis siblings and their many friends to gather to swim, fish or simply frolic like children like to do.

Linwood Cemetery was another favorite nearby destination for the local kids. The historic graveyard, which was established in 1894, essentially recounts the history of Macon's African-American community with the people interred there. Roughly

4,000 people are buried within the cemetery's 13 acres, including Buffalo Soldiers, Spanish-American war veterans and Jefferson Long, the first African-American from Georgia to serve in the U.S. Congress.

But history would have no bearing on the decision by Rodney Davis and his friends to go there to play on so many afternoons. Located just a few minutes' walk from the Davis home on Neal Avenue, the cemetery was a well-manicured sanctuary of sorts where the neighborhood kids could cut loose all they wanted and let their imaginations run freely away from the prying eyes of adults. It was only appropriate that Rodney Davis' final resting place would be where he had enjoyed so many fond memories during his youth.

Flying kites was always among their favorite pastimes at Linwood Cemetery, even if it did take some creativity on their parts to make the kites themselves from items at home because they usually lacked the money necessary to buy them commercially.

But it was the backyard that had always been Rodney's unquestioned kingdom, the place where he so readily exercised all the freedoms of a curious mind that had been heavily inspired by the many movies he'd taken in. He was at his happiest when swinging from old tires strung up on tree limbs, jumping from roof tops like the many daring cowboys he'd long idolized from the big screen or wavering without a care or concern from limb to limb just like he'd watched Tarzan of The Jungle do it on so many occasions.

He and Gordon had inherited their love of the outdoors from their two doting grandfathers. Poppa, as their paternal grandfather was affectionately called, had counseled his grandsons beginning at a very early age in the importance of always respecting the outdoors and in using, respecting and taking proper care of guns.

As a sign of their maturity and faith in his own abiding trust in them, Poppa presented both Gordon and Rodney with their own 20-gauge, single-barrel shotguns for their 10th birthdays.

They were heady days for sure for the two brothers, frolicking alongside one another from one new adventure to the next. The brothers faithfully completed their household chores on time and were usually way too busy always playing outside during whatever free time they had to manage to land themselves into too much trouble with their parents.

But their exuberance would be interrupted from time to time, however, such as the day when his mother found little Rodney cowering in bed in the middle of the day. She immediately began to worry that something was amiss because Rodney was never the type to retreat to his room while there was still daylight outside unless something was awry.

"What's wrong with you?" she asked.

"I broke my neck," Rodney gently uttered, his bed covers muffling a voice now weakened by pain.

"You did what?" Ruth Amanda Davis asked back, the worry in her voice now starting to become more apparent. "Start over from the beginning and tell me what happened."

The episode was just one of the many that characterized the childhood of a fearless little boy who would do anything to keep up alongside his older brother.

During one of his other many escapades with his Gordon, Rodney had fallen out of a big tree in his grandmother's yard and landed on his head. Fortunately, he wasn't bleeding nor had he broken the skin or any bones, but he was more than just a little sore.

His anxious parents rushed him to the nearby emergency room at the local hospital, where doctors told them that their son would be just fine after taking some aspirin and getting some rest.

Rodney had fallen while he and Gordon were busy stockpiling small rocks in the tree to throw at innocent passersby. The two mischievous youths enjoyed the high vantage point because they could easily toss the stones while remaining unseen by their intended victims thanks to the fullness of the large evergreen tree in which they were hiding.

They had been preparing a stash to hoist up the tree to always have ready to fling at their future intended targets when the loaded five-gallon bucket Rodney had been dangling from his arm suddenly became too heavy. He quickly lost his balance and plummeted head-first the 10 or so feet down to the hard ground.

Rodney never cried, but quickly retreated home to his bedroom, where his worried mother soon found him.

"I'm just glad you weren't hurt seriously," she said, "but let this be a lesson to you. You and your brother had no business climbing up into trees so as to throw rocks at people passing by. You both know better than that. You could have really hurt somebody and yourselves."

"Yes, ma'am," Rodney sheepishly replied. "I won't ever do that again."

It wasn't long, however, following his return from the emergency room before Rodney was back alongside his older brother and climbing the tree again, the pain and discomfort from his previous fall quickly forgotten. No little mishap here or tiny scratch there was going to keep him from keeping up with Gordon.

Giving up at anything was never an option.

Rodney had shown the same such spiritedness some time earlier after running full speed into a barbed wire fence and badly cutting up his face. He, Gordon and the family's white terrier dog had been playfully chasing a horse that belonged to a neighbor when the owner returned home unexpectedly one afternoon.

"What are you boys doing?" he bellowed upon discovering the young intruders. "Get off my property right now!"

Not that he had to ask twice. The brothers had immediately taken off upon seeing him, with Gordon reaching the barbed wire fence first before slowing down and carefully going through it.

"C'mon, Rod! Hurry!" Gordon pleaded of his brother.

Unsure what was behind him, Rodney had been looking backwards as he had begun sprinting away just behind his brother. He was so immersed in all that was happening behind him that he had just begun turning his head to the front when he suddenly slammed into the barbed wire at full speed, suffering a deep gash above his left eye.

"Aaaaaaagggh!" he screamed out in agony, seeing the blood on his right hand after placing it on the wound to gauge its severity.

Gordon had already begun sprinting away, sure that his younger brother was still just right behind him when he heard his scream.

"You okay?" Gordon asked after coming to a sudden stop to see what had happened. "What happened?"

Rodney was in too much pain to go into much detail at that point, but wasn't about to slow down with their angry neighbor closing in.

"I'll be OK, Gordon," he said. "Let's just get out of here first."

Rodney managed to limp home, but the sheets on his bed were already soaked with blood by the time his mother returned home and whisked him to the emergency room to receive stitches to stop the profuse bleeding.

But three days later, Rodney, Gordon and the family dog were back at it and out chasing the horse again.

But his days as a budding masterful military mind or daring cowboy, however, would have to wait because Rodney's mother had long been a strong advocate for education. Her own life circumstances had cut short Ruth Amanda Davis' own formal education, but she was determined her children would not miss out on the precious opportunities that came with schooling.

The nearby St. Peter Claver School perfectly fit the bill for everything for which Ruth Amanda and Gordon Davis, Sr. were looking for their children. The culturally diverse Catholic school had been founded in the early 20th century as a place in Central Georgia that would serve as a religious and educational foundation for African-American children. It soon became a pillar of better education for African-American kids in Macon, molding the values and ethics of impressionable children from preschool to eighth grade while also offering the kind of strong spiritual development the Davis family was seeking.

Located just a short walk from the Davis home on Neal Avenue, the school encouraged academic excellence as much as civic responsibility.

They were lessons Rodney Davis and his siblings took to heart.

It soon became apparent that Ruth Amanda Davis' passion for education had been passed down to Rodney, who thrived in school from the outset as the delight of his kindergarten class. He loved school and was likewise revered by everybody there. So carried away by Rodney's enthusiasm from a "great" day at school, his father once asked his son, "What did you learn at school today?"

"I can beat everybody in my class!" Rodney proudly proclaimed in response.

"At what?" Gordon Davis, Sr. asked.

"At everything!" his son answered back.

His impromptu declaration as class champion in all things earned him the nickname of "Bully," a handle that would follow him the rest of his life.

Rodney, though, was hardly the type of bully whose connotations immediately conjured a number of negative images. Rather, he instead grew to be known as a Robin Hood-type bully, one who was always quick to champion the rights of the underdog, those he believed less able to protect themselves.

As he later did for his younger siblings while coming of age in the ugly Jim Crow era. And as he later also did in Vietnam for his fellow Marines.

Always doing right by others just seemed to come naturally to Rodney. He especially cared about those closest to him, and had derived his strong sense of loyalty and sense of duty from his father, whose sterling example was there for him to see every day.

Gordon Davis, Sr. worked long, often grueling hours as a building contractor to provide for his family, usually coming home tired and often malodorous from his long day's hard labors. Nothing would get his devoted wife in a huff quicker than when he would nonchalantly park himself into his Lazy-Boy chair in the living room without first showering and changing clothes.

But no matter how tired he was, the Davis patriarch made sure to never shirk his household responsibilities. Either to his children or his wife.

That included faithfully attending church each Sunday morning at First Baptist Church, and doing considerably more than just sitting in the pews. Being actively involved in the church was imperative for the entire family. Despite the trying social climate of the times outside their home, the Davis family had long felt very blessed to have one another and always looked to give thanks to God.

Located in Macon's downtown just a few blocks away from City Hall, First Baptist had been serving the city's black community prior to the end of slavery nearly 100 years earlier. It had often served as the sanctuary to which local African-Americans could turn for spiritual uplifting in the battles, first against slavery and later Jim Crow. The church had a long history of serving as the site of many civic meetings to combat racial inequities.

Religion had long played a major role within the African-American community, dating back to the days of slavery. It was often a lone pillar of hope and inspiration in dark times. Things were hardly perfect yet, but thanking God for the many blessings they did have was very important to both of Rodney Davis' parents.

"Did you pray on it?" Granny would often ask when one of her children or extended members of her family came to her with a problem.

God always came first in the Davis household, followed by a deep love of family. So staying at home on Sunday mornings and not attending church was never an option.

"You could have been sick, but you were going to church," Gordon Davis recalled.

The family patriarch, Gordon Davis, Sr., had long been active at First Baptist Church, and was held in very high regard within the community in his prominent role as a deacon.

He made sure his sons would follow suit. So it wasn't long before Gordon Davis, Jr. and Rodney were old enough to thank God in their own way for all their blessings by joining the kids choir that practiced once each week and later serving as ushers. Their younger siblings would later do likewise when they became old enough.

Like most youths their age, Gordon and Rodney would have preferred playing outdoors at all times if left up to them, but the two brothers didn't ever mind doing anything just as long as they were doing it together.

The two boys were literally like two peas from the same pod. Wherever one might have been found, it was a good bet the other was usually never far away. Theirs was a very special relationship, a deep bond more reminiscent of the closest of best friends as well as brothers, and it would always remain that way.

Their love for one another had always been unconditional, with the two never having any secrets between them. Their special relationship empowered them both to dare do just about anything while growing up because they knew the other one would always be there with unconditional support.

"In my whole life, I have never had to worry about a cheering squad," Gordon Davis said. "I have never been able to do anything wrong in his eyes. As his big brother, it didn't matter what I did.

"Most people just talk about having special relationships like that. But we always knew that somebody had your back. We never worried about what was going on around us because I didn't have any question who was on my side."

But nobody else always enjoyed the same kind of pass always afforded Gordon.

Rodney at times had a quick temper, and sometimes it would get the best of him. It was a side of him that could endear him to as many people, as it could also probably sometimes rub them the wrong way. His mother and father had often discussed the issue with him, and Rodney did his best to stay calm during any argument that might have arisen rather than let his fists go and do the talking for him.

But it wasn't always easy, and he didn't always succeed.

It was early on high school that Rodney and one of his closest friends began debating some inconsequential matter one afternoon. The talk between the two eventually amped up as neither would concede their point. Things had become heated when suddenly Rodney's temper won out and he began swinging away at his good friend.

The two were quickly separated, and Rodney soon made the sincerest of amends, but the incident filled him with great remorse and stuck with him for a long time. He remained forever cognizant about the need to always do better about keeping his temper in check.

Even if it weren't always that easy to do while growing up under Jim Crow.

But there eventually came a second turn of major events that would also upset young Rodney.

Baby brother, Howard, became the latest addition to the family in 1949. Gordon, Jr. and Rodney had been together through thick and thin for all of Rodney's first seven years, so Howard's arrival initially came as a thorn or sorts in Rodney's side. He soon adopted a hardline attitude towards this second person who had suddenly displaced him even further away from his beloved mother.

In fact, Rodney often asked, "When were the people coming back to get this baby? He's been in the house long enough."

"That's your baby brother," Ruth Amanda would say in return, "so be nice to him."

Howard gradually won Rodney's acceptance - usually, however, as the object of play - and life would go on.

Saturday mornings were always special in the Davis family as Poppa always took the two oldest boys to town and allowed them to be boys.

"Go on to the movies and wait 'til I come get you," Poppa would say as they rounded the corner with the Hart Building in sight on the corner of Cotton Avenue and Second Street.

The movie theater was located on nearby Broadway. While Poppa worked, "Hugh's Boys", as the people on the streets came to know them, just walked all about, going in and out of different shops. At the movies, Hugh's Boys were allowed to run a "tab", eating candy, popcorn and the like until Poppa arrived. He'd pay, pick the boys up and they would start the long walk back to their home in Macon's Pleasant Hill community in the dark.

The downtown post office at the corner of Mulberry and Second Streets had always been one of the favorite stop-over destinations for Hugh's Boys on any given Saturday. Rodney would often stand outside for what seemed like hours, mesmerized by the iconic oversized recruiting poster on the sidewalk outside that proclaimed, "Uncle Sam Wants You!

The young man would stand almost breathlessly while gazing at the various military men in their distinct uniforms – Army, Navy and Air Force. But it was the striking image of the sharply-clad Marine in his dress blue attire in particular that had always captured Rodney's eye and his active imagination.

He was just 12 years old when he first stopped in front of the poster and declared to his big brother Gordon one day, "I am going to be a Marine."

CHAPTER 4

COMING OF AGE IN THE JIM CROW SOUTH

Racist edicts first enacted in the United States in 1876 to disenfranchise the freed former slaves, the so-called "Jim Crow" laws found largely in the South were state and local decrees that legitimized racial segregation in all public facilities, including public schools, public places and public transportation, and mandated the forced segregation of restrooms and restaurants for whites and blacks.

The term "Jim Crow" is a line from a minstrel song from 1835.

In many instances, African-Americans were even denied their most basic of civil liberties, such as the right to cast a vote, often through the dubious pretext of things such as poll taxes and literacy tests.

The shameful period in American history supposedly included a "separate but equal" status for African-Americans, but the reality was that it led to second-class treatment and accommodations that were almost always inferior to those provided to white Americans, thereby institutionalizing a number of economic, educational and social disadvantages.

Emboldened by such laws passed by the states, many private Southern businesses, political parties, unions and other private organizations would create their own Jim Crow arrangements at the various local levels, barring blacks from buying homes in certain neighborhoods, from shopping or working in certain stores or from working in certain trades.

By the early 20th century, the stifling Jim Crow laws had effectively denied African-Americans opportunities and had become a major impetus behind their subsequent Great Migration to northern cities such as Chicago.

The white establishment that was responsible for the codes justified their actions by pointing to their alleged superiority over the black race. Mixing the races in any sort of manner was never God's intention and would just bring problems, they said.

There were no exceptions to be made, not even during wartime.

The city of Macon shamefully treated German and Italian prisoners of war being housed at the nearby Army base at Camp Wheeler during World War II much more cordially than its own African-American residents. A small number of Japanese prisoners were also at the camp, although they were not white and therefore did not enjoy the same overall treatment as their European partners from the Axis Alliance.

The camp was among the more than 500 spread across America, including the 24 branch camps throughout south and central Georgia. The first 2,000 of the former enemy combatants began arriving at Camp Wheeler in Macon's outskirts by early 1944.

Named in honor of Confederate general Joseph Wheeler, the more than 14,000–acre facility had originally served as a U.S. Army training site during World War I. The advent of Second World War meant it had to be converted into use for POWs by late 1943 as England began running out of the necessary space needed to house the prisoners.

Some of the captured soldiers worked as mechanics, typewriter experts and tailors, but most were put to work as day laborers in the local sawmill or farm areas, accruing wages of about 80 cents per day. The prisoners were paid in currency that could only be used at the camp, but were supplied with more than enough adequate food, sleeping quarters and medical care. They were even permitted education opportunities while incarcerated and allowed to display national symbols of pride and to conduct funerals with military honors for their deceased comrades, said Dr. Antonio Thompson, the Austin Peay State University history professor who authored the 2010 book, "Men in German Uniform: POWs in America during World War II."

By mid-1944, their shirts emblazoned with a large letters "PW" had become a familiar sight throughout the Macon area and the sites of the many other such POW camps throughout Georgia. Some German and Italian POWs eventually began befriending soldiers and local farmers, and, in some cases, were later invited into the homes of Americans for meals and entertainment.

Yet any such acceptance remained among the remotest of possibilities for African-Americans at that time.

Despite their POW status, the former enemy combatants were still held in higher regard than African-Americans at the time. The late William P. Randall was a Macon contractor charged with overseeing Italian prisoners as they labored on various work projects inside Camp Wheeler. Imagine the sheer dismay and deep anger he and his fellow African-American colleagues felt when the captured enemy soldiers were consistently welcomed into the camp mess hall to eat following the day's conclusion, while they were told to go elsewhere. Randall would later recall the unsavory events to his kids, telling them how deeply the shoddy treatment angered him and his colleagues and how it spoke volumes about the state of race relations in Macon and elsewhere.

"In 1940s America, racial issues were very much alive and Jim Crow was definitely an issue in the South," Thompson said.

Yet the local attitudes towards race were never more apparent than during the occasions the African-American soldiers guarding the prisoners needed to adequately feed them per requirements of the Geneva Convention. The black soldiers, many of whom had previously served overseas, usually brought food with them to eat prior to leaving the base for work assignments or had made prior arrangements with local farmers to feed the prisoners. But on the occasions they didn't, they were forced to stop for food at some of the local restaurants in downtown Macon.

Only the uniformed African-American soldiers weren't allowed into the restaurants to pick up the food, Thompson said. Not even under such unique circumstances. A white German or Italian POW was instead sent into the establishment to pick up the food before coming back out.

The sad reality was that, in Macon and elsewhere throughout the South especially, their white skin even trumped the fact that they were prisoners from a country with which America was then at war and that many likely had American or Allied blood on their hands, given the fact they were captured on the battlefields of North Africa. Racism in the region was apparently strong enough to even supersede patriotism.

It's hardly surprising then that a significant number of former German POWs would go home upon their release and speak of how well they were treated in U.S. before later returning to Georgia to live out their lives following World War II's conclusion.

It hardly seems fair, but life in Macon at that time was hardly fair to those not of white skin.

Usually strictly enforced throughout the South, Jim Crow had already become a de facto way of life in Macon and many other places by the time Rodney Davis and his siblings began really coming of age in the 1950s and '60s. So much so that many African-Americans fearful of later violent reprisals, cynical of any realistic chances of affecting change or just resigned to the only treatment they had ever known simply accepted the shabby inferior treatment as simply the status quo.

Notorious "Whites Only" and "Colored" signs were commonplace in Macon and throughout the South at the fronts of many stores, restaurants, public bathrooms and even public water fountains. Complete white domination of state and local law enforcement and judicial bodies only further served to help the oppressive system keep Macon's African-American community in a stranglehold, one designed to always make them feel inferior as the Davis boys grew up in the 1950s.

Rodney M. Davis would later go on to become his hometown's most renowned war hero, lauded in such haughty places like the White House for his bravery and tireless devotion to his country and the men with whom he proudly served. But Jim

Crow had a specific name in mind for him and other African-Americans who only sought to be treated fairly in the nation they also loved and called home.

Nigger.

At the time the Davis brothers began to come of age, Macon was still much like the rest of Georgia and much of the South in that it was particularly steeped in Jim Crow and strongly resistant to change and racial progress.

There had been some incremental steps, but progress continued to be agonizingly slow for the likes of the Davis family and other African-Americans in coming in Georgia and throughout the Deep South. In Georgia, segregationists weren't about to sit quietly following the Supreme Court's landmark 1954 Brown vs. Board of Education decision that said segregation in public schools was unconstitutional.

Nearly two years after the ruling in 1956, Richard Russell, an influential U.S. Senator from Georgia, became one of the architects of a paper informally known as "The Southern Manifesto," which attacked the Supreme Court's decision as judicial overreach. Russell, who penned the final version after watching staunch South Carolina segregationist Strom Thurmond author the original draft, was among the entire Congressional delegations from Georgia, Alabama, Arkansas, Louisiana, Mississippi and Virginia to sign the document.

"This unwarranted exercise of power by the Court, contrary to the Constitution, is creating chaos and confusion in the States principally affected," the document says in reference to the Supreme Court's Brown vs. Board of Education decision. "It is destroying the amicable relations between the white and Negro races that have been created through 90 years of patient effort by the good people of both races. It has planted hatred and suspicion where there has been heretofore friendship and understanding."

As if to further make the state's official point, Georgia changed its state flag in 1956, reverting back to a previous version that included the same Confederate Battle Flag used by the Confederate States of America, as well as various white supremacy groups.

It would remain the state's official flag until 2001, serving formal notice that Georgia wasn't giving segregation up without a fight.

Segregated life was ugly and it was humiliating, but it was the only world Rodney and his brothers knew at the time. As such, Rodney Davis and many others would regularly endure the kind of daily indignities and other humiliations that no American citizen should ever have to bear, the kind that would stay with them forever. Their every trip out beyond the friendly confines of the family home proved to be an adventure with the ugly specter of racism and the violence often associated with it ever present.

The local Woolworth department store and the city's renowned Nu-Way hotdog joint are where the Davis boys often liked to eat when downtown. Woolworth's was well known for its scrumptious hamburgers, while the to-die-for chili-covered hotdogs and all their tasty accompanying trappings offered at Nu-Way were easily considered the best in town by Rodney Davis and his brothers, Gordon and Howard.

The sweet taste from either of the mouth-watering food joints was considered the most delicious culinary treat there was, so stopping by and satisfying their appetites whenever possible was always considered a privilege to which they always looked forward.

But doing so also brought humiliating constant reminders of their second-class status in the eyes of their own hometown.

The Woolworth's boasted a cute dining counter in the store's front, where its favored white patrons could leisurely sit, eat and take in the scenic view of all that was going on in the city's quaint downtown area. African-Americans, however, were not afforded even that simple right at the time, relegated instead to eating in the back of the store in the cramped and dilapidated quarters reserved for them.

Located just a stone's throw away from City Hall, Nu Way's cozy dine-in area consisted of roughly 10 counter stools and seven additional snug booths for customers. There was no better place to sit and enjoy the savory ambiance that accompanied the chain's celebrated bright-red hotdogs that came heavily draped in onions, ketchup and Nu-Way's own special chili sauce, the likes of which made customers consistently come back craving for more.

But the inside dining area and its booths were off-limits to hungry African-Americans. So the Davis brothers and others were forced to stand outside when visiting, awaiting their food to instead be brought out to them to be eaten elsewhere as the restaurant's white patrons regularly ate inside in contrasting comfort.

African-Americans were allowed inside at some other dining spots in the city, but they were forced to stand in a special line designated for them. Upon receiving their food, they had always been under strict orders to take it somewhere else to eat. Their money was OK, but their presence was decidedly not welcome.

The local police would quickly be called if anybody dared to think otherwise, and were quick to physically enforce the racist edicts if needed.

Not even the popular Dairy Queen and its exclusive outdoor facilities in the city's downtown were exempt. Customers visiting the popular ice cream chain were to place their orders at the window in front before sitting outside in the separate "White" and "Negro" areas designated for the two different races.

Rodney, Gordon and Howard Davis often talked amongst themselves about the ugliness of it all, how wrong it was that they and other African-Americans were being treated. Each instance made them angry and always ready to lash out in retaliation, but equally as frustrated because they felt helpless to do anything about it by themselves.

"Is it ever going to get any better?" Rodney asked Gordon on a number of occasions. "I don't like being treated like this, like I'm somehow not as good as a white man. It just ain't right. I'm as good as anybody."

Gordon did his best to assuage his brother's growing frustration with the situation.

"Man, it's gotta get better," he would say. "They can't keep treating us this way forever. It just takes a lot of time before things change in Macon. We just gotta be patient."

"My patience only goes so far," Rodney would often say in return.

****

Despite the adverse social conditions of the era, Rodney thrived in high school, playing varsity basketball, varsity football and the clarinet in the school band while making many close friends along the way.

Blessed with great height, excellent speed and soft hands, he was a standout wide receiver who played football and served as an effective post player in basketball. His older brother says that he has no doubts that Rodney could have played collegiately at either sport had he so chosen.

Now a magistrate judge and a former state lawmaker, William C. "Billy" Randall recalled his Appling High School classmate's athletic abilities just a little differently, but spoke reverently of his memories of his childhood friend.

Rodney M. Davis' senior picture at Appling High School in 1961. (photo courtesy of the Davis family)

"Rodney was a really good guy who could get along with anybody and he was always joking and making us laugh," Randall said. "I don't know anybody who didn't like him. He wasn't the most coordinated guy in the world, but, with his height, he didn't have to be. He'd always control the boards when we played basketball."

The Randall family lived nearby on Grant Avenue and has been particularly close to the Davises for several generations. Their family patriarch, William P. "Daddy Bill" Randall, was a prominent spokesperson and community leader for Macon's black population and ranked as one of the city's most influential civil rights activists. He actively served as a chief board member of Macon's NAACP and as chairman of the Negro Citizens Negotiating Committee, the African-American civil rights organization established in the city during the early 1960s that played a prominent role in the pivotal 1962 Macon bus boycott.

Rodney and Billy Randall thrived among a circle of close friends who had all grown up together in Pleasant Hill, doing what normal teenagers like to do during those critical coming-of-age years. If not often rushing home each day after school to play basketball and other sports, they could always be found enjoying one another's company at the bi-weekly dances held at the nearby Booker T. Washington Community Center on Wednesday and Friday evenings that attracted African-American teenagers from all over Macon.

His friends say Davis' above-average height, olive-brown skin and fine grade of jet-black hair proved popular with the girls.

Sunday nights usually meant gathering at the J.D.'s Soda Shop to hang out for a little while longer in a last-ditch effort to relax with friends and avoid the burden of school and other daily responsibilities for as long as possible.

But just returning to school would always pose their own set of conundrums for Rodney Davis and his friends. In addition to the expected academic challenges, Davis and his friends faced the added problem of Macon's Jim Crow laws that made their daily lives even more difficult.

That's because African-Americans in Macon and other places at the time were not allowed to ride the traditional yellow school buses that picked up students and carried them to and from school free of charge like their white counterparts.

The city of Macon had instead worked out an arrangement with a local transit company to pick up African-American children. Davis and others were forced to pay for those services each week or find alternative ways to school.

But they managed despite the obstacles set before them, and Rodney Davis soon began sticking out at school for reasons well beyond his height.

Those who knew him in high school said his quiet and easy-going temperament belayed the strong will and likeable personality that made him a natural leader.

"He was always the one to say 'I'll do it,' and organize the other students," Eddye Mae Booth, Davis' history and American government teacher at Appling, was quoted as saying in a May 1983 Macon Telegraph article. "It was something about his personality that attracted students. They trusted and respected him."

Jessie Williams was a high school classmate who first met Rodney Davis when the two were high school sophomores and vividly remembers their first meeting. The two shared several classes together and quickly became fast friends.

"He was tall, slim and lanky, but he was an easy-going guy and was smiling all the time," said Williams, who enlisted in the Army after graduating from high school, but did not go to Vietnam. "Everybody liked Rodney. He was a real good dude."

His disposition was a naturally quiet one even among his friends, so much so that even many who knew him best said they were stunned to later hear of the heroic circumstances of his death in Vietnam some years later.

"They say the Marines make a man out of you," "Billy" Randall said. "Apparently, that's what they did."

Williams left the Army in 1968, but was bitterly disappointed to learn upon his return to Macon that the city in which he had grown up had not changed much since he had left. He had only been home a short time when he and a group of friends tried to go to the nearby Macon Health Center to work out and play basketball with the area's many other veterans who regularly congregated there.

Only Williams and his friends were denied admission into the facility.

"Ya'll ain't allowed here," they were told by a white front desk clerk. "Ya'll can't come in here."

Outraged that they had just proudly finished serving the country they all loved only to be treated so rudely back in their own hometown, Williams and the others held their ground and refused to leave. The police were called and promptly arrested Williams and everybody with him.

"I really felt like busting that dude," said Williams, who refuses to go back to the Macon Health Center even to this day.

It was only after getting out of jail later and reflecting upon the ugly incident that Williams got to thinking more about his good friend Rodney M. Davis. About how his good friend willingly sacrificed his own life for the simplest of rights not even afforded to him and those who looked like him right there in Macon.

"[The incident] gave me mixed emotions [about how Rodney died]," he admitted.

Now a distinguished math professor at Mercer University, Charles Roberts grew up in Macon and knew Howard Davis from their childhood school days together. He also endured his share of racial indignities while growing up and again later after becoming one of the first African-Americans to enroll at Mercer when he did so in the fall of 1965.

Roberts was still in college in 1966 and Rodney Davis in London when Atlanta-based civil rights activist Hosea Williams came to Macon with the intent of leading a peaceful march from First Baptist Church to nearby City Hall to demand full equality.

The protesters had just departed the church when Macon police and sheriff's deputies surrounded them with their guns drawn. A single misstep on anybody's part was all it would have taken for a bloodbath to have taken place on Macon's downtown streets.

"Some of them were waiting, hoping to get a chance to take a shot at us," Roberts recalled.

It was for such deep-seeded reasons that Roberts was later stunned to hear of the unique circumstances surrounding Rodney Davis' death in Vietnam.

"To me, it was amazing [that he gave his life for five white Marines]," Roberts said. "These were people he barely knew and they had oppressed us for hundreds of years. He was definitely a hero."

Gordon Davis says there's no question his younger brother would have not tolerated such racially-motivated slights or put up with the indignities from anti-war protestors had he survived the war and returned to Macon.

"I would like to have seen someone dare call him a nigger or try to spit on him while he was in his uniform," Gordon Davis said. "Rodney would have broken their jaw."

****

The two oldest Davis brothers were still in high school when they first came to the realization that they and others like them could make a difference after all. They were among a large group of local African-Americans who descended upon downtown

Macon to picket Woolworth's for its discriminatory policies. Their peaceful protests and encouragement of a boycott of the retail chain helped to soon bring about change and fair treatment for African-Americans at the downtown store.

But there was still widespread discrimination the Davis brothers and other African-Americans were forced to endure on a daily basis. The reality left them frustrated beyond measure, and unsure as to what else to do.

Though far from idyllic, life in Macon was the only world they knew. So the Davis brothers were left clinging to only the hope that things would eventually get better someday.

Yet they often wondered.

How could the same people who so shamefully denied them their full civil rights claim to have loved America, yet simultaneously have such contempt for a different group of their fellow Americans? It never made any sense to the Davis siblings.

But Gordon Davis, Sr. and his wife had done their best to shield their children as much as possible from all that was happening around them as they raised them. They made sure none of their five children ever went to sleep hungry or feeling poorly about themselves in any way even in the ugly face of Jim Crow. They were taught to always stand proud. White people seeking to collect rent, insurance money or any other kinds of bill payments were never allowed to enter the Davis home, much like African-Americans were generally not allowed in most white homes throughout Macon.

His home was his castle, and the Davis family patriarch demanded it always be a safe and positive environment for his family.

Gordon Davis, Sr., whose work as a contractor had brought him into close contact with many of Macon's prominent white residents, even made it a point on various occasions to take his children to eat at virtually every restaurant in town, attend virtually every church in town and even visit the city's lily-white Elks Club, all despite segregationist ordinances that had been specifically passed to prevent them from doing so.

Nobody ever said as much as a word to the head of the Davis family about it, although he likely understood that it was his deep connections about town that helped make such allowances possible for his family. Gordon Davis, Sr. was cognizant that not many others within Macon's African-American community were afforded even that much.

His wife, Ruth Amanda Davis, was also a beneficiary of her husband's sterling professional and personal standing within the community. Granny had become an endearing fixture in her own right throughout the community over the years, beloved by both the black folks and white folks alike who knew her. Her engaging personality and perhaps a skin tone light enough to almost pass for white were probably among the biggest factors in her landing a job in a women's clothing store in downtown Macon starting in the late 1960s.

Granny was not only an extremely popular employee at the store even as racial tensions boiled everywhere else, but her children and, later, even her grandchildren were always warmly greeted when they came into the store to greet her.

"They loved her and always welcomed her kids," Howard Davis said.

But the ugly reality of Jim Crow was never far off, and careful consideration of its possible ramifications was always a necessity.

The Davis family happened to be downtown attending a Christmas parade one year in the early 1960s when young Robert and Debra suddenly complained to their father of being cold and hungry. With no concern about any possible repercussions, Gordon Davis, Sr. waltzed into a nearby restaurant with his children in tow – probably to the shock and dismay of some of the white customers sitting inside – so they might be accommodated.

His intent was to make sure his children never felt inferior to anyone. It was a lesson his children would carry with them the rest of their lives.

"You're as good as anybody," the family patriarch often told his children. "Don't you ever forget it!"

But life in Macon at that time was what it was, and the ugly specter of racism was never far away.

But the two older Davis siblings were eager to play even a small role in helping to make daily life in Macon better for those who looked like them. While in high school, Gordon and Rodney had regularly attended the many tense NAACP meetings held at First Baptist Church, listening quietly as older, more seasoned members of Macon's African-American community plotted out their responses to the deep-rooted institutional racism they faced. The two brothers were never shy with their own opinions, but were always careful to make sure their parents knew everything that was going on and everything in which they were involved.

Gordon Davis, Sr. and Ruth Amanda Davis knew all too well of the dangers to which the brave protesters were exposing themselves in their fight for equality, so they had to make sure their sons were taking no unnecessary risks with their participation in a number of sit-ins and other peaceful forms of protests.

"Who are you going with? What are you going to do? How far are you willing to go? What are you going to do in the event that something crazy happens?" were just some of the many questions they had to have satisfactorily answered before giving their sons their OK.

Peaceful change is what they preferred, but the two oldest Davis children had their own, often more preferred method of dealing with Jim Crow when confrontation was unavoidable.

Gordon was getting ready to begin college at Fort Valley State University, but his younger brother and constant sidekick was still in high school on June 8, 1959 when a racist salesman provoked Rodney and received a beating for his troubles. The two teenaged Davis brothers had driven across town when Gordon parked the car and ran into a friend's apartment for what was supposed to be just a few minutes.

Rodney was sitting quietly in the front passenger seat when a white man selling various merchandise from the back of his own vehicle first approached. Unable to park any closer to where he had desired because of the Davis car and the presence of a nearby ice cream truck, the salesman bellowed at Rodney to get out of his way.

"Hey, boy, move that car!" he shouted. "And do it right now. I got stuff to do!"

Rodney wasn't sure what to do at first, sitting still without uttering a word in the hopes that his older brother would be right back out and the whole misunderstanding would simply blow over without incident.

But that wasn't to be.

Becoming increasingly upset by the second that a black man had the temerity to not only refuse his request, but ignore him altogether, the white salesmen angrily repeated his ugly catcall for Rodney to move the car.

"Boy, did you hear me?" he barked.

Rodney knew he had to respond at that point, so he simply replied that he didn't have the car keys, and that his older brother would be back out in just a minute. The white driver of the ice cream truck then chimed in, saying he would be pulling away shortly and that his space would be available.

The matter should have been over, but the white salesmen wasn't about to let a nigger's insolence go unchecked. Angry this young black man didn't know his place, the racist salesman rejected the overture, saying, "No, I want this boy to move."

Rodney continued to sit quietly in the car without budging.

"Boy, you must not have heard me!" he shouted at Rodney as he approached the Davis car.

The offending man then made the mistake of sticking his head inside the rolled down passenger side window with more derogatory words when Rodney suddenly grabbed him, yanked him inside the car and beat him silly with a flurry of hard punches to the face.

He had tried to stay calm, but had been pushed beyond his limit by the overbearing racist salesman. Rodney was irate now with his temperature running high, so he had little tolerance even for the heavyset black woman who lived nearby and had just witnessed the unsavory events.

She had begun screaming aloud, "You hit that white man! You hit that white man!" when Rodney Davis jumped out of the car and quickly quieted her obnoxious noise as well with a firm slap to the face that put her on the ground.

He'd clearly gone way too far when he struck the woman, no matter her submissive mentality that somehow deemed it always permissible for white folks to mistreat African-Americans at their leisure.

The police quickly arrived on the scene, however, and promptly arrested Rodney for interfering with police. It's unclear why they chose that particular charge.

Gordon Davis quickly rushed home to alert his mother so they both could immediately head to the local police station where Rodney had been taken. Ruth Amanda Davis was soon at the station's front desk, demanding to know about her young son's whereabouts when a police officer then threatened to arrest her and Gordon for "being sassy."

"Go right ahead," Ruth Amanda Davis dared him. "I'm not going anywhere until I see my son and I know that he's OK."

The police officer arrested both Granny and her oldest son Gordon on the spot.

Gordon Davis, Sr. became irate after receiving word of what had happened and wasted little time in reaching out to a very prominent, white Macon attorney he knew for help. It wasn't long afterwards that the Macon police had a quick change of heart and promptly released the three detained Davis family members after hearing from the well-regarded attorney who would be representing them.

Charges against Rodney Davis were soon dismissed as well when the racist salesman failed to identify him as his assailant. Gordon Davis now looks back at the incident with great pride as the defining moment that he, his brother and their mother all defiantly stood up for themselves and refused to bow to Jim Crow.

"When you don't treat yourself like you were second class, you don't allow other people to treat you like second class," he said.

But the brothers' sometimes more preferred and much more direct way to deal with Jim Crow was never more apparent than during a sit-in training session they were attending later in the spring of 1961. Designed to emulate the successful sit-ins that had begun in Greensboro, N.C. a year earlier to help usher in integration at lunch counters throughout the South, the training exercise was intended to prepare the eager young people for the different kinds of indignities and ugly slights they would likely have to endure while trying to make a positive change.

Such as being called all kinds of nasty names and even spat upon. Or worse.

One of the session's liberal white organizers had just come behind a seated Rodney Davis, clearing his throat and preparing to spit upon him when Rodney suddenly jumped up and knocked the trainer down with a hard blow to the face.

"Nobody ever spits on me!" he snapped at the stunned man now lying at his feet. "Under no circumstances ever!"

It wasn't exactly the turn-the-other-cheek type of pacifism for which organizers had been looking, so both Davis brothers were politely asked to leave.

"We couldn't do that," Gordon Davis said, laughing now as he recalled the story. "We could take care of the folks on the corner with those sticks hopping on the Freedom Riders. We knew how to take care of that."

And they enjoyed that more aggressive approach, too, perhaps mostly as a welcome release from the ugly way they had been treated by the country they loved. So much so that the brothers and a few of their thrill-seeking friends would at times drive out into the rural Macon suburbs on some afternoons in search of the Klan members rumored to have been in the vicinity.

It was probably a good thing for all parties potentially involved that they never came across any.

But not everybody shared that same courage in the face of systemic oppression.

Many local African-Americans at the time did their best to just steer clear of white folks almost entirely as Macon, just like so many others at the time throughout the Deep South, was virtually segregated in every sense.

Theirs were two entirely different worlds altogether.

African-Americans weren't allowed to even enter the same door as whites when going to see a doctor. There were always separate waiting rooms for the races, and white patients were almost always treated first.

Founded by the son of a former slave, the Douglass was the movie theater reserved for African-American patrons, while whites enjoyed two separate downtown venues at the Bibb and Capitol theaters. The Douglass helped cement Macon's lofty status at the time as one of the places to be for entertainers. Duke Ellington and Cab Calloway made appearances, while the venue was also where Otis Redding got his start and even later welcomed such luminaries as Little Richard and James Brown in the 1960s.

But segregation made no such allowances even for such distinctive artistic talents as theirs.

As dictated by local ordinances, even Macon's many cemeteries were divided along strict racial lines, with separate places of permanent rest designated for blacks and others for whites.

The same held true for public schools as both black male and female African-American students in Macon attended the much older, more worn-down and overcrowded high school at Ballard-Hudson. Some like Rodney Davis would later matriculate to Peter G. Appling High School when it opened. Meanwhile, white male students attended Lanier High School, while the white girls went to a sister school at the nearby Miller High School. Both white schools benefitted greatly from the decidedly better facilities, newer textbooks and a more generous school budget.

But interaction couldn't be helped sometimes, as Macon is a relatively small town with everything fairly close together.

The Davis family home on Neal Avenue sits in the city's predominantly black Pleasant Hill section of town, but the community borders other, wealthier nearby white neighborhoods as well.

Problems would often arise when the two segregated worlds were suddenly mixed.

White residents displeased with the sight of the Davis brothers or other African-Americans minding their own business while walking down their sidewalks en route to school or anywhere else were almost always quick to let their disapproval be known with their many racially-charged catcalls.

But just one shout of "Nigger" was usually all it took for Rodney Davis to come out swinging with both fists, emerging victorious almost every time. Words were just that, but young Rodney and his older brother were not about to sit idly by while others disrespected them or their siblings.

Their deep pride and strong sense of right and wrong wouldn't allow it. And they were more than willing to fight if necessary to make their point. Some things, the two brothers agreed, were worth fighting for.

"It was [Rodney] and I against the world," Gordon Davis said. "We sent a whole lot of crackas to the hospital."

Reports of the tall black kid's fighting prowess soon spread, eventually leading Rodney to a confrontation with an equally tall white youth from Lanier one afternoon. A basketball star at his own school, the big redhead had been recruited to specifically come to that part of town and face off against this Rodney Davis he had heard so much about. His own size and well-known pugilistic skills had led the cocky redhead and others to believe he was more than a match for any black kid who dared oppose him.

He quickly found out otherwise, and never gave Rodney Davis or any of his brothers any more problems. For good measure and to make sure similar incidents never happened again, Rodney made sure to have a few choice words with the nearby white students who had recruited the big redhead in the first place.

"Do it again, and you're gonna answer to me," he warned them.

They never did.

Rodney, however, also took home his own share of cuts, scrapes and black eyes to show for his efforts.

Yet, sometimes it appeared even to his own siblings that he might have also relished the many physical confrontations, perhaps his own way of lashing out in return against Jim Crow's oppression.

Or maybe it was always because what Rodney was really fighting for extended well beyond just him.

It was always about respect, and he was keenly aware that it always had to be earned rather than given. It was an illuminating life lesson that Rodney took to heart and would remember the rest of his days.

Some of the same youths Rodney would fight one day went on to become his friends soon afterwards. Those who didn't at least came away with a grudging respect for him and knew better than to ever cross him ever again.

But Rodney and the rest of the Davis brothers didn't always fight their way through the white neighborhoods. They would run away as fast as they could on other occasions, especially when white residents would unleash their German Shepherd attack dogs on them for simply having the temerity to walk on sidewalks in their communities.

Get busy fighting or get busy running. Nothing came easy under Jim Crow.

Not even the seemingly innocuous daily task of completing the daily paper route the Davis brothers shared just a short walk from the family home would escape the ubiquitous specter of racism. Gordon, Rodney and Howard Davis would dutifully leave their house and arrive together each day at the Macon Telegraph's nearby distribution center well before sunrise, picking up their papers before delivering each one and then heading off to school. It was a job the brothers began in elementary school and would continue doing throughout high school.

Only they were forced to stand and wait outside in the dark for their papers to eventually be handed to them, as African-Americans were not allowed inside the building. It made for some long, bitter cold mornings in the winter months and left little doubt among Gordon, Rodney and Howard Davis that segregation in Macon was definitely a 24/7/365 phenomena.

In fact, it was so deeply imbedded in the city at the time that the Macon Telegraph went through the added time and expense of printing different community editions each day, one for the white community and another for the black community. The newspaper's odious practice lasted until the early 1970s.

No African-Americans were usually ever listed in the paper's wedding or engagement announcements.

But things could have been worse still, said Dr. Andrew Manis, a local professor at Macon State College and the author of "Macon Black and White: An Unutterable Separation in the American Century."

While clearly far from ideal, the racial climate in Macon was certainly better than that of many other places throughout the Deep South, most notably in the relatively nearby Ku Klux Klan strongholds of Alabama and Mississippi.

The Klan hadn't been that all strong in Macon since the 1950s, Manis said, crediting the presence of Macon's three colleges —

Mercer University, Macon State and Wesleyan College - and a relatively progressive editorial board at The Macon Telegraph for having prevented things from spiraling even further towards the radical fringe.

Yet, that was hardly any consolation to those forced to live with the many daily indignities they endured in Macon under Jim Crow.

It was all somewhat perplexing to Rodney and his brothers at times because they had come up as children playing alongside many of these same white teenagers and young people now calling them nasty racial epithets.

Hate and racial intolerance, as the Davis brothers quickly deduced, isn't an inherited trait, as much as it is a learned behavior.

And like many other African-Americans at the time, the Davis children were determined to never allow the ignorance, fear and prejudices of others to win out. They loved their hometown of Macon and felt an abiding allegiance to their country, no matter its faults. Proudly serving his country with the Marines had long been Rodney's dream.

But it would be a while longer still before things got better in Macon.

According to Manis, the racial climate in the city had begun to take a turn for the worse by the early 1960s in the wake of a string of empowering national victories by the national Civil Rights Movement such as the Montgomery bus boycott precipitated by the arrest of Rose Parks in 1955, the forced integration of schools in Little Rock, Arkansas in 1957 and the successful 1960 sit-ins in Greensboro, North Carolina that forced the integration of that city's lunch counters.

The leader of the Montgomery bus boycott, Dr. Martin Luther King, Jr., had visited Macon in September 1957, speaking to a crowd of roughly 600 people at Steward Chapel African Methodist Episcopal Church.

King, who would go on to head the national Civil Rights Movement, challenged the city's black community to make its voices heard by voting.

Segregation was on its last legs, but African-Americans still had a long ways to go at that point before achieving full equality as citizens in America, King warned, according to a September 19, 1957 account in the Macon Telegraph.

Other civil rights successes throughout Georgia soon followed his visit to Macon. In Savannah, African-Americans staged a 19-month boycott of white owned merchants from March 1960 to October 1961 before the city finally agreed to desegregate a number of public facilities.

In January 1961, Charlayne Hunter and Hamilton Jones integrated the University of Georgia when Macon-based U.S. District Court Judge William Bootle ordered them admitted. The first two students of color to enroll at the state's flagship university arrived in Athens to hateful student chants of "Two, four, six, eight! We don't want to integrate!"

A racist mob attacked their dorm following a basketball game on campus a few days later and had to be driven off by police tear gas. Instead of punishing the white rioters, UGA suspended Holmes and Hunter "for their own safety and the safety of other students."

It was later revealed that some university and state government officials had hoped to repeat the tactic that had worked for the University of Alabama when it expelled its first African-American student, Autherine Lucy, following a white riot on the university's Tuscaloosa campus in 1956.

But the measure didn't work in Georgia as more than 400 university faculty members signed a resolution condemning both the violence and the suspension, and calling for the return of the two black students.

Both Hunter and Holmes soon returned to class, but their struggle was very telling about the state of race relations in Georgia at the time. Then a high school senior, Rodney Davis and his friends were captivated like most of Macon and the rest of the state by all that was happening in Athens. Nobody, however, was all that surprised.

But like many within Macon's African-American community, the Davis brothers couldn't comprehend at the time why anybody would intentionally subject themselves to such ugly overt racism, not to mention the threat of violence on a daily basis by seeking to attend the University of Georgia.

"Why the heck would she even WANT to attend the University of Georgia?" Rodney would sometimes ask some of his friends. "Why would any black person ever even want to go to school there?"

Rodney already had his own plans to enlist in the Marines following graduation, even if his parents still didn't know as much at the time. Attending the University of Georgia wasn't something he would have chosen, but he had long felt strongly about his right and that of others looking like him to be able to attend the state's flagship university if they ever so desired.

The local NAACP in Macon immediately jumped into action, wasting no time in calling the city's black community together to prepare for whatever outcome awaited. Everybody eagerly awaited the outcome, and all were pleased when Hunter and Holmes soon returned to campus and began their ground-breaking education.

The Davis brothers joined other African-Americans in Macon and throughout Georgia in their pleasure with the outcome, believing that if integration had come to the state's marquee site of higher learning, then it was sure to soon follow throughout the rest of the state.

"We thought if we could go to the University of Georgia, then we could go anywhere," Howard Davis said.

But it would be a while still before that became a reality.

Things hit closer to home in Macon in 1962 with an effective bus boycott that ultimately achieved its aims of integrating city and county buses and increasing the employment of African-Americans as bus drivers and mechanics.

Led by a number of Macon-area pastors, the boycott of the Bibb Transit Company began on Feb. 12, 1962 and lasted for three weeks. Despite a series of court decisions in other Georgia cities that had declared segregated transportation unconstitutional, Macon's African-American residents had still faced massive resistance to integration efforts.

Student protesters and ministers had been arrested after attempting to sit in the front seats of Bibb Transit's buses. They hoped their planned embargo of Macon's buses would expedite things.

The boycotters enlisted Donald L. Hollowell, the renowned civil rights attorney who had served on the legal team for Charlayne Hunter and Hamilton Jones, to file suits in the federal and state court systems on their behalf. Wallace Miller, Jr., who represented the Bibb Transit Company, tried to strike back by imposing a restraining order on the leaders of the boycott, but that move failed to deter the civil rights activists.

On March 2, 1962, Bootle declared segregated bus seating laws unconstitutional, and ordered the Bibb Transit Company to comply with his ruling. The Macon bus boycott ended two days later.

Fearful of change and their own status in the new world order they knew to be coming, many whites in Macon and elsewhere nationally had become increasingly frustrated by the successes of the Civil Rights Movement and what they perceived as too many gains, too quickly for African-Americans.

So they began to lash out in retaliation.

Sometimes in the form of violence.

Mostly, however, they began overwhelmingly siding with very conservative political candidates who promised to tow a hard line against the progress that civil rights leaders were demanding immediately.

People like Barry Goldwater and Richard M. Nixon in the presidential elections of 1964 and 1968, respectively. And locals like Ronnie W. Thompson.

The racial tension had become poisonous in Macon by May 1962, so much so that one day a group of white city residents affiliated with the KKK felt emboldened enough to grab a mentally challenged black man who had become familiar sight in Macon's downtown and buy him a one-way bus ticket to Detroit. In a note to Jerome Cavanaugh, the Motor City's liberal white mayor, the White Citizens Council stated that the 40-something-year-old homeless man nicknamed "Bullfrog" was a "typical black person" who should join Detroit's many other unemployed African-Americans.

The segregationists mockingly called their act "a one-way freedom ride."

Ironically, "Bullfrog", whose real name was Archie Campbell, was eventually brought back to Macon, thanks in large part to the efforts of Thompson, the city's fiery and staunchly conservative future two-term mayor.

Thompson, who served as the city's head from 1967 – 1975, tried to assure Cavanaugh that such actions didn't represent how most of Macon's citizens felt. The racially-charged incident, however, immediately drew major national headlines and only served to further cast the city in an unfavorable light.

The ongoing national civil rights movement would again be the talk of all of Macon while riveting the rest of the nation as well later in the fall of 1962 when Air Force veteran James Meredith would become the first African-American to attend the University of Mississippi.

A riot by thousands of angry segregationists ensued following Meredith's court-ordered admission into the school, prompting President John F. Kennedy to send in federal troops and U.S. Marshalls to assure his safety while getting an education.

The tense showdown was the talk of the entire nation, dominating conversations everywhere, Macon included.

"It was all over the news," Howard Davis recalled. "It was in all the papers and in everything. That's all everybody was talking about."

Each highly-publicized event just served to ratchet up the racial tensions in Macon even further.

Locally, racial divisions in the Macon area would also again nearly come to a head a few months later as a fight broke out on April 1, 1963 as black youths attempted to integrate one of Macon's segregated parks. White youths retaliated at Tattnall Square Park the following day, attacking blacks with sticks and rocks before local police interceded and ended the violence.

Mayor Ed Wilson responded to the escalating racial upheaval by closing the park.

The incident at the park reflected the growing divide among the Macon's black and white youth as the bitter struggle for civil rights and the growing violence had polarized all sides, filtering all the way down to kids who had grown up playing alongside one another without incident over the years.

There were pockets of areas within Macon where black and white kids continued to play full-court basketball together in relative harmony, but it was understood that racial tensions were always near the surface. All it would usually take was one heated game and nasty racial epithets, fights and bottle-throwing incidents soon followed. Angry that they'd lost a highly-contested game, some white players would sometime hide in the nearby woods until dusk before launching a cascade of glass bottles at the courts where the black players were still playing, said Howard Davis.

"Sometimes we would throw some back at them, other times we just hauled ass," he said.

There were other incidents as well, as some of the black teenagers aware of the daily struggles for equality called themselves doing their part by heading to white neighborhoods to play basketball and make their own points. The ensuing fights that often resulted were their way of defying Jim Crow.

It was obvious that racial tensions were running extremely high in Macon much like everywhere else. It wasn't uncommon for black families to be awakened in the middle of the night to find crosses burning in their yards, said Ronnie Mays, Sr., a childhood friend of the Davis children who also went on to serve in Vietnam with the U.S. Army.

The perpetrators of such heinous acts in Macon often weren't officially Klan members, Mays said, but they relied on the widespread fear of the organization to accomplish their objective and drive home their point of intimidation.

Mays, however, said he refused, however, to give in to the fear and animosity that was the source of so much of the malevolence.

"It was rough," he said, "but I knew that hate for hate, that wasn't the answer."

Rodney Davis was serving in the Marine Corps at Camp Lejeune, N.C. by then, but his thoughts were always of his family back home. He had to know they were safe from the social upheaval gripping the nation, but especially the Deep South.

"Is everybody OK?" he'd ask his parents during his weekly phone calls home. "I heard about some of the stuff going on. This is just crazy."

"Don't you worry about us, Rod," his parents would always make sure to tell him in their efforts to reassure him of their own well-being. "We'll be just fine. You just make sure you take care of yourself."

A large of number of African-Americans from Macon boarded buses for the long ride to Washington, D.C. a few months later and were the estimated 250,000 people in attendance at Dr. King's iconic "I Have a Dream" speech on Aug. 28, 1963. King's moving words and the unquestioned symbolism of delivering them on the steps of the Lincoln Memorial served to perhaps make that day the defining moment of the Civil Rights Movement.

The activists each returned home pleased, clinging to the hope that change was soon coming.

But the same racial tensions would again serve to ratchet up several notches to unprecedented levels in Macon and everywhere else throughout the South shortly afterwards following the bombing of the Sixteenth Street Baptist Church in Birmingham, Alabama on Sept. 15, 1963, killing four young black girls who had been attending Sunday school and wounding 23 others.

The church had been used by civil rights leaders as a meeting place in their efforts to register voters in Birmingham, a city perhaps more notoriously entrenched in segregation than any other in America.

The violence not only shocked the nation, but carried large international ramifications as well for a U.S. government that was suddenly open to hypocrisy charges as it strongly advocated for human rights and freedom for suppressed peoples overseas.

Civil rights advocates blamed George Wallace, Alabama's segregationist governor, for fostering the toxic racial climate that allowed for such hate. A week before the bombing, Wallace had told the New York Times that to stop integration, Alabama needed a "few first-class funerals."

A witness identified Robert Chambliss, a member of the Ku Klux Klan, as the man who placed the bomb under the church steps. He was soon arrested and charged with murder and possessing a box of 122 sticks of dynamite without a permit. On Oct. 8, 1963, Chambliss was found not guilty of murder, but was instead fined $100 and given a paltry six-month jail sentence for having the dynamite.

He was later convicted of one count of murder in 1977, and would remain there until his death in 1985. It would be decades later before others who conspired in the plan with him would also be brought to justice.

Worried about the spread of the growing violence to their own town as tempers boiled over, anxious officials in Macon joined local African-American leaders in urging calm in the tragedy's aftermath.

Macon, like so many other places throughout the South at the time, was a powder keg in need of just the slightest spark to go off.

But the deaths of four innocent teenaged girls and the subsequent injustices slapped in the face of those trying to find their killers stirred the nation's consciousness like never before and spurred the federal government into more decisive action. The bigoted Jim Crow laws were eventually rolled back, starting with the passing of the 24th Amendment on January 23, 1964 that eliminated the nefarious poll taxes that had been designed to prevent African-Americans from voting by requiring them to pay a fee to vote.

Georgia, however, remains among the eight states that have never ratified the amendment.

The subsequent Civil Rights Act of 1964 and the Voting Rights Act of 1965 helped do away with the remaining vestiges of the Jim Crow laws. Signed into law by President Lyndon B. Johnson on July 2, 1964, the landmark Civil Rights Act was the most sweeping civil rights legislation since Reconstruction, prohibiting discrimination of all kinds based on race, color, religion or national origin. The decree also provided the federal government with the teeth needed to enforce desegregation.

Officials in Macon quickly began to make the changes needed to comply with the new civil rights legislation, while antsy local African-American leaders continued to urge calm in the meantime.

There was again a newfound optimism that things might be improving, but, as had been the case on previous occasions, it didn't last long.

Any doubt there was still a long ways to go was answered a little more than a month later in early August 1964 when the decayed bodies of three young civil rights workers in Mississippi – two white, one black – were discovered in an earthen dam roughly six weeks after they'd disappeared in late June. The three had been working to register black voters when they had been arrested on trumped-up speeding charges, incarcerated for several hours and later released into a KKK ambush to be brutally murdered.

Closer to home, a decorated African-American World War II hero had been killed by the KKK just north of Athens, Georgia on July 11, 1964. Lt. Colonel Lemuel Penn, an Army Reservist who had been awarded the Bronze Star for bravery, was driving home to Washington, D.C. from Fort Stewart with two other black officers when Klan members opened fire on their car.

Two local men were arrested for the heinous act a few weeks later, but a jury of 12 white men needed just 81 minutes to acquit both Klansmen on September 4. The federal government would later convict the men on federal charges stemming from violation of the Civil Rights Act that had just been passed nine days prior to Penn's murder, but it appeared to many as if it were open season on African-Americans in Georgia.

The cumulative result was that racial tensions were now running higher than ever before everywhere, as Jim Crow wasn't about to give up without a fight. The prospect of widespread racial violence was now very real.

In late September 1964, Macon's black residents went to court to contest the continued segregation of Baconsfield Park, which had been willed to the city by A.O. Bacon. In his last will, the late U.S. Senator and former Confederate veteran decreed the park to be for whites only and held in trust by the city.

Local black citizens of Macon later challenged the Georgia Supreme Court's 1966 ruling that kept the park segregated. The U.S. Supreme Court eventually overturned the decision and forced the park's integration, saying in 1970 that the park was public in nature and that its "whites only" status violated the Equal Protection Clause under Fourteenth Amendment.

The city of Macon was forced to relinquish its trustee status in order to comply with civil rights legislation. Talk of the racial confrontation was on everybody's lips in Macon and Rodney Davis continued to have his own questions about happenings back home as well.

"Are you guys OK?" was usually the first words out of his mouth during weekly calls home.

And he was always told the same thing every time be broached the subject.

"We're fine," his parents would always say. "You just take care of yourself and be safe."

Yet, unlike several other cities throughout the rest of Georgia, Macon had few angry confrontations between its police and African-Americans demanding full equality during the late 1960s and '70s. The city eventually did away with segregation in public facilities without the violence or national media attention that had characterized the civil rights movements in other nearby locales such as Atlanta, Albany and Americus.

The integration of schools in Macon was another matter, however, and wouldn't come until years later.

The majority of Macon's civil rights activists opted for what they viewed as more consensus-building efforts and negotiations with city and county officials to resolve disputes and implement affirmative action programs.

In addition to desegregating public facilities, they also sought to improve salaries and other workplace conditions for African-Americans and other minorities, while also increasing access to state and county jobs.

But actual progress, however, remained very slow in coming to Macon even by the time Thompson had taken office two months after Davis' death in Vietnam in 1967. The city's African-American police officers, for example, were still subject to overt discrimination, handicapped with longer work hours than their white counterparts and a lack of paid holiday leave or even clothing allowances, Thompson said. Macon's black police officers were still not allowed to ride in city police vehicles by the time he assumed power in November 1967. It remained that way until the Georgia General Assembly mandated otherwise in the early 1970s.

Macon, Georgia as a whole was staunchly entrenched in maintaining the status quo, and still needed additional major prodding for change to happen.

Mercer University student Sam Oni quickly learned as much in 1963 when he became the first black student to enroll at the school. Born in what is now Ghana, Oni was still in his native land when he first came into contact with Southern Baptist missionaries and eventually chose to go to the United States for his college education.

Mercer officials deliberated for more than a year whether Oni should even be admitted, he told a captive audience during a February 2011 visit back to Macon for the school's Founder's Day festivities.

Oni was eventually accepted and chose to enroll at Mercer anyway, despite having been encouraged to instead attend either Morehouse College in Atlanta or Lincoln University in Pennsylvania.

Arriving as the civil rights struggle was beginning to heat up, he said he found the American Dream he'd heard so much about while growing up and the reality of life in Macon to be completely different.

White students unaccustomed to attending schools alongside others of color were mostly hostile to him, largely avoiding as much as making eye contact with him or even speaking to him upon his arrival.

He was often showered with racial epithets.

Donald Baxter, a white sophomore, had been asked to be Oni's roommate. Baxter hesitated at first, but grudgingly accepted, and the two men hit it off right away.

The experience would help open Baxter's eyes like never before to what life in Macon was like for people of color. He recalled being shocked when Clifton Forrester, the pastor of the Tattnall Square Baptist Church that sat on Mercer University property, visited both he and Oni, telling them that Oni would not be welcome to worship there.

Baxter said that he, too, had been subject to venomous racial slurs because of his friendship with Oni.

"For the first time, I knew what it was like to be black and Sam Oni," Baxter was quoted as saying in the Macon Telegraph.

Oni would later in 1966 challenge a local church located near the campus on its policy of barring membership to African-Americans. Oni, who had broken the color barrier at Mercer three years earlier, had been inspired to stand up against the segregationist edict after hearing that members of Tattnall Square Baptist Church had previously voted almost three to one to close the doors of the church to blacks.

He tried to enter the church for worship services on Sept. 25, 1966, only to be physically prevented from entering the building by two church deacons and arrested by police. Church members later voted to fire the pastor who had befriended Oni and encouraged his non-violent civil disobedience.

It wasn't until years later that Tattnall Square Baptist Church finally became integrated.

Macon, however, was hardly alone in Georgia even then with its lack of real progress in race relations as the years passed. Perhaps nothing spoke more volumes about the state of affairs than the January 1967 inauguration of unapologetic segregationist Lester Maddox as the state's governor.

Swept into office in the November 1966 election by widespread dissatisfaction with desegregation and the Civil Rights Act of 1964, Maddox had made a national name for himself and endeared himself to many white Georgians a year earlier when he chose to shutter his own Atlanta restaurant rather than desegregate.

His election only further emboldened the many in Georgia still resisting change.

Recalcitrant Bibb County school officials in Macon would only finally comply with school integration after a court order in 1971, prompting thousands of irate white residents to protest - with Maddox himself in attendance - some 17 years following the Supreme Court's breakthrough Brown vs. Board of Education decision.

Many angry white residents would subsequently pull their children from Macon's public schools and form their own private schools rather than allow them to attend integrated ones.

Such resistance to progress should hardly come as a surprise in a state that didn't even formally ratify the 19th Amendment that guaranteed women the right to vote until 1970, some 50 years after it became a federal law.

It seemed as if there would never be any escaping the polarizing issue of race in Macon or anywhere else throughout Georgia.

Rodney M. Davis had been able to witness a small number of the many happenings in person as he had come home to Macon on leave only a few times throughout much of the early- to mid-1960s. The Davis family didn't have the kind of money it took for him to return home on every leave, so Rodney usually just either stayed on base or found somewhere else closer by and more affordable for him to visit during his free time. Nonetheless, he always remained cognizant of what was happening back in his hometown and throughout the South while he was away, and how it affected his family members and others he deeply cared about on a daily basis.

It worried him greatly.

But Davis had already begun focusing all of his time and energy into becoming the best Marine he could be, and had soon pretty much stopped discussing such matters with his brothers by that point. The brothers had also stopped dwelling on such matters because it was the only world they knew. That's just the way things were, and they figured they couldn't change things by themselves.

"We just have to be patient," they would keep telling themselves. "Things are going to change."

The problem, as the Davis brothers and many others saw it, wasn't with them, as much as it was with those whose intolerant views were causing the problems. They never felt inferior or bad about themselves in the slightest way and refused to let their present situation drag them down. They continued to take at least some small consolation in knowing that things in Georgia would eventually improve.

Or at least so they hoped.

But other Macon natives from that era have since been very critical of that kind of passive thinking, attributing the city's excruciatingly slow progress towards racial equality in some small part to an African-American community that was way too passive and accommodating to the white establishment.

C. Jack Ellis grew up in Macon and would go on to become the city's first African-American mayor when he was elected in 1997 to the first of his two four-year terms. Ellis lived in the city's all-black Unionville enclave across town and knew of Rodney M. Davis, although he did not know him personally.

Ellis, who fell short in later bids to again get elected as Macon's mayor, cited the lack of a historically black college in Macon as another reason for the considerably slower march towards change than seen in other areas throughout Georgia and the rest of the nation. Brave students from the Historically Black Colleges and Universities (HBCUs) such as Morehouse College and Spellman College had long been among the forefront in the push for full equality in nearby places such as Atlanta, Savannah and Albany.

Their energy, passion and willingness to even risk physical harm rather than wait any further for only equal treatment in their own country helped spur the growing civil rights movement to new heights, Ellis said.

But Rodney Davis' focus had been largely elsewhere by this point. After initially leaving Macon, the Marines had become the primary focus of his life, and he had begun dealing with heated racial issues of his own even within the ranks of the U.S. military.

But Macon would always be his home, and he deeply loved it and all of America, no matter its faults.

In 2008, the U.S. Congress formally apologized to African-Americans for both slavery and the Jim Crow laws that fostered de facto segregation, calling the two "stains on what is the greatest nation on the face of the Earth and the greatest government ever conceived by man," according to a speech given on floor of the House of Representatives by Congressman Steve Cohen, a Democrat from Tennessee.

To this day, Georgia has refused to formally apologize for its role in Jim Crow.

CHAPTER 5

LOOKING OUT FOR
HIS OWN

Rodney Davis' unbreakable allegiances to his family and to his friends had always been well beyond reproach. Unquestioned loyalty to those closest to him was a trait he held dearly.

That included his family first and foremost. By the time Rodney had reached high school, his parents had already welcomed two more children to the family with the arrival of Robert in 1952 and then Debra two years later.

Because of their differences in age, Rodney quickly became more like a surrogate father of sorts to the two than just an older brother, but all the more so later after Gordon went away to college. Rodney was constantly looking after their well-being, not to mention some of his mother's many younger nieces and nephews who would also stay with the Davis family for various periods of time on occasion to form what quickly became a very large extended family.

As such, one of Gordon, Sr. and Ruth Amanda Davis' primary tenets was that all their children always look out for one another. Rodney Davis took that charge very seriously.

"He was not the oldest, but he was the biggest," Howard Davis recalled. "He took control of things. He was THE big brother. He always felt like he should protect everybody."

Howard Davis openly admired both his older brothers and desperately tried to keep up with both Rodney and Gordon. By the time the two older Davis brothers had become licensed drivers, Howard was trying to do that, too. It wasn't long before Rodney would begin taking his little brother with him on occasional rides down the street, allowing an excited Howard to sit in his lap and steer the car.

It meant the world for Howard to do as his brothers did. He would often tag along with Gordon and Rodney every morning to help them out on their paper route. Robert and Debra were still too young to come along early on, so they remained at home.

The three older Davis brothers always enjoyed spending time with one another, and it was a relatively easy way for all of them to make a little money for themselves as well each day before heading off to school.

It was dark when they'd leave the house, but they didn't mind as long as they were together.

Robert Davis soon became old enough himself and began joining his brothers on the route each morning. He was still just a small child, but there was never any doubt that his older brothers would always have his back in any eventuality. That was the way all the Davis siblings had been raised.

Family always looked after one another.

"Rodney didn't care what you did," Robert Davis recalled. "If you were his brother, you were his brother. It didn't matter what you did. He was always with you."

Delivering papers was a way for the brothers to make some easy spending money while spending time alongside one another, but it was hardly always easy. In addition to the early hours that made for some long days for each of the brothers, there was also the matter of dealing with the petty rivalries and competitive fires that were the result of the opening of the new high school for the city's black students.

Ballard-Hudson had long been the city's lone high school for African-American students, but the opening of the new Peter G. Appling High School in 1958 meant that Ballard now had a nearby natural rival, pitting students from Pleasant Hill against one another in sports and everything else. That competition wasn't always friendly, and the Davis brothers soon discovered that the rivalry extended to those delivering the newspapers throughout the area as well.

It wasn't uncommon for the testosterone-fueled boys gathering in the pre-dawn dark to collect their newspapers to soon begin having choice words among themselves. Things would quickly escalate. There were plenty of other occasions when the Davis brothers would bring their family dog with them for extra companionship. Many of the other local boys delivering paper did likewise and some of the dogs would inevitably begin fighting among themselves on occasion, leading to more fighting among the boys in charge of looking after them.

"The dogs started fighting and we started fighting, too," Robert Davis said.

Whatever the reason for the fight, Gordon and Rodney Davis' first thoughts were always to young Robert and Howard. The two youngest Davis brothers were quickly shown to a secure hiding place with very clear instructions from their older brothers to stay hidden there until the melee had run its course.

Gordon and Rodney, however, weren't about to back down, but looking after their brothers would always be their most immediate concern.

The brothers would often be finishing up their route in the city's Pleasant Hill section when other youths would be beginning to first make their way outside while also en route to school. It wasn't uncommon for Rodney to bark out something at strangers he believed to be looking funny at him and his brothers or perhaps even just watching a little too close.

"Whattya looking at?" he would bellow. "We gonna have a problem?"

It didn't matter who it was because Rodney Davis never backed down from anybody. Especially when it came to his siblings.

The same held true following church each Sunday in the summer, when Rodney would walk young Howard, Robert and Debra to the nearby store for ice cream. He would insist his siblings march in front of him, so that he might always have them in his sight while simultaneously surveying all potential hazards coming ahead.

It was a noble gesture, even if it did make things a little uncomfortable at first for his two younger brothers and sister. They were all much, much shorter than their very determined, 6-foot-5-inch older brother and sometimes struggled at times just to maintain the long strides needed to consistently stay in front of him.

They naturally chafed at first, but Rodney insisted they do as told. It was for their own well-being, he explained.

That worked just fine most of the time as just the sight of someone of Rodney's unusual height and length was often enough to dissuade potential trouble-makers. But Rodney stood more than ready if it didn't.

That's because what he may have lacked in pure physical girth, he more than atoned for with heart and a little creativity. Tall but paper-thin, Rodney would often sport two wallets in his rear pants pockets along with an occasional folded up newspaper, all in the hopes of projecting a more physically imposing stature that would further deter any would-be aggressors from messing with him or those under his watch.

He had no problem literally taking matters into own hands if that didn't work.

The Davis children (l to r -(front) Debra, Howard and Robert; (back) Gordon, Rodney) (photo courtesy of the Davis family)

To mess with his siblings was to mess with him, and he would have none of that. There was never any doubt Rodney would always do whatever it took to protect them.

And that held true probably more for Gordon more than anybody. They were best friends who just happened to be brothers and were usually never far from one another's side. So anybody who dared mess with his older brother immediately drew Rodney's wrath.

The two boys were still in high school one evening when a stranger made the mistake of intentionally stepping on the new leather shoes Gordon had worn for the teenage dance the two brothers were attending. Gordon was proud of his new shoes and had chosen this particular occasion to break them in as part of his ensemble.

The Davises had just arrived a few minutes earlier when another teenaged boy nonchalantly cut in front of Gordon, marching all over his shoes without as much as bothering to look around as he continued on his way.

"Hey, man!" Gordon shouted at him. "What the hell are you doing?"

The guy stopped and suddenly turned around, unapologetic in the least.

"What? You have a problem?" he asked.

The words had no sooner come out of his mouth when Rodney exploded up like a rocket from the nearby table in which he was sitting and listening, flooring the offending boy with a blow to the face from his closed right hand.

Gordon never had any more problems with that kid ever again and the two brothers enjoyed the rest of their evening without further incident.

"I never saw him back down from a fight or anything derogatory that was said," Howard Davis said.

Howard Davis often refers to an illuminating story of his own about his older brother that took place as Howard had just begun high school sometime in the early 1960s. He had been visiting a girl from across town with whom he was smitten one day when a group of boys standing outside a nearby store began pelting him with bottles before chasing him home.

Rodney just happened to be home on temporary leave from Camp Lejeune in North Carolina when a bruised and slightly scratched-up Howard walked through the door.

"What happened to you?" Rodney asked.

"Some boys across town," Howard said. "I was over visiting this girl and they didn't much like my being there."

"Oh, is that right?" Rodney said. "We'll just see about that."

"Don't worry about it – I'll be alright," Howard said, trying to deflate the situation.

"Hell, no, I do worry about it," Rodney shot back. "Nobody does that to MY brother."

Rather than just letting the matter go, a determined Rodney insisted his younger brother join him in the car. They were headed back across town, resolute in their determination to find the offending party and make things right.

Howard joined his brother, but was hardly enthusiastic about doing so. He knew there had been roughly 10 boys who had chased him home, and he wasn't sure just how he and Rodney alone were going to settle the score.

Howard was content just to leave well enough alone at that point, but he knew deep down that his older brother's strong sense of right and wrong wasn't about to let that happen.

"Don't worry about it, man," Howard Davis unsuccessfully pleaded with his older brother. "It ain't no big deal and I didn't get hurt. Seriously, Rod. It ain't even worth going back over there."

But doing anything otherwise wasn't even a thought with Rodney.

Although he could have possibly jeopardized his own budding military career, he just knew he wasn't going to stand idly by while someone messed with his younger brother. Something had to be done about it and done immediately or it would likely happen again.

Some things were worth the fight.

"C'mon, Howard!" he snapped as he began heading out the door. "You can't let people disrespect you like that! You gotta let 'em know that you ain't no punk! Now get your ass in the car and let's go!"

All eyes turned on the two Davis brothers as the family's black 1958 Mercury slowly pulled up in front of the store where the cross-town bullies were still congregated.

It didn't take long for Rodney to exit the vehicle and make his intentions clear.

"Who's been messing with my brother?" he demanded as he jumped out of the car, unmoved by the group's superior numbers.

A melee immediately ensued, with Rodney beating down most of the offending boys and more than getting his licks in on several others as well. In successfully defending his brother, he made certain none of those same boys ever bothered Howard or anybody else in his family ever again. His honor, that of his brother and his own desire to always do right by others less able to fend for themselves were easily worth a few minor scrapes and bruises.

That strong sense of unquestioned loyalty especially applied to Gordon. The two had been especially close since childhood, and Rodney was determined that nobody was going to ever do wrong by his older brother.

Under any circumstances.

It was for that very same reason Gordon, Jr. and Rodney Davis would find themselves in another memorable physical exchange a few years later, this time just prior to Rodney's deployment to Vietnam in 1967.

Rodney had just returned home for the first time in a while, enjoying a month's leave before heading out to Southeast Asia. He had brought his new wife and their two infant children home with him to Macon for the first time, making for a joyous homecoming for everybody.

He and his older brother were out about town, enjoying each other's company and that of their respective wives one evening when the ugly specter of racism reared its ugly head again. The Davis' car had come to a halt at a stop light with the window down when a car carrying several young white men pulled up alongside theirs. The white men suddenly began making derogatory comments towards the two brothers before then disrespecting their wives by whistling and jeering at them.

Josephine Davis was sitting in the back seat, doing her best to calm the blind rage she knew to be quickly building both inside her own husband and Rodney, who was seated in the front passenger seat beside his older brother. Both men's wives sat in the back.

"Don't worry about it, Gordon," she pleaded. "Just let it go and let's forget about them. It isn't worth it."

"Let it go?" Gordon retorted. "Hell, no! Ain't nobody gonna not only disrespect me, but then disrespect my wife in my presence. White man or not. What kinda man would I be if I just let that go? Awww, hell no."

The offending white men began speeding off when the light turned green, never even thinking for one second that there might be physical repercussions from their rude and unprovoked actions. They just assumed the Davis brothers were going to sit idly by and quietly take such treatment because that was the way things were at the time in Macon for the most part.

They assumed wrongly.

Ignoring the repeated pleas from their worried wives seated in the backseat to avoid any trouble and to just let the matter go, Gordon Davis quickly accelerated, catching up to the car with the rude segregationists before signaling to them by hand that they needed to pull off to the side of the road. Both brothers immediately began climbing out of the car upon their stop, instructing their wives to stay where they were.

"We'll be right back," Gordon Davis said as he quickly began making his way out of the car.

Strong words were then exchanged, as the men from the two cars also got out and squared off for a confrontation. The subsequent fight didn't last long, as Gordon and Rodney easily won the day and gave the two white men some much-deserved attitude readjustment.

"Betcha they won't do that again," Rodney said to his older brother as they made their way back to their vehicle, not even bothering to hide the wide grin across his face.

No way the two very proud brothers were ever going to allow anyone to talk to them in that manner, let alone to their wives. To get beat down in a fight is one thing, but both men considered doing nothing to be even worse and much more stigmatizing.

A real man always stands up for himself, his family and those closest to him, they believed.

Those who knew Rodney were hardly surprised, especially after his having become a very proud Marine. That's just the way he'd been raised, his siblings said.

"He truly was a man of the people," his sister, Debra Ray, recalled. "If you got a problem, it was his problem, and he was going to take care of it."

So it would be later again for Rodney Davis, only this time with his new brothers of the U.S. Marine Corps.

CHAPTER 6
THE MAKING OF A MARINE

Rodney M. Davis graduated from Peter G. Appling High School on May 29, 1961.

He'd long talked about joining the Marines, but most of his family had just naturally assumed it was just that, and that he would instead follow in the footsteps of his older brother Gordon, who had gone on to attend nearby Fort Valley State University.

But Rodney had big plans of his own.

His deep affinity for the Marine Corps had always beckoned. That long-held fantasy and his own worry that his parents wouldn't be able to financially afford sending both him and Gordon off to college at the same time are what prompted him to enlist in a four-year stint with the U.S. Marine Corps in the summer of 1961.

He had already signed the necessary paperwork and returned home when he announced what he'd done to his mother and father later that evening. The news was something neither of his parents had ever really expected, so they initially listened in somewhat shock as Rodney began telling them what the decision would soon mean for him.

Rodney's siblings mostly sat in stunned silence, unsure how their parents would react once their initial astonishment wore off.

All except his older brother Gordon.

He had been there those many years earlier when his younger brother first proclaimed his intention to someday be a U.S. Marine. And it was Gordon to whom Rodney had always confided about everything, including his intentions to enlist. His later decision to marry would mark the first and only time in his life that Rodney had not previously sought Gordon's opinion on a major decision.

So Gordon could only wish his brother the very best because he knew better than most that there was never any going back once Rodney had made up his mind on something.

Their parents would eventually take the news in stride. A contractor who consistently worked long days to support his family, Gordon Davis, Sr. never became angry and, instead, calmly heard out his son's case for his decision. The former Navy man could probably better understand than most his son's burning desire to test his own mettle like never before and to get out from the relatively small confines of Macon and see the world.

Granny, as Ruth Amanda Davis had come to later be affectionately known, was another story entirely.

She was somewhat upset initially with Rodney's decision because she had just always assumed that all of her children would be attending college. She had long preached about education being something that nobody could ever take from them, about how it would continue reaping dividends for them throughout their lives.

It's not that Ruth Amanda Davis ever had anything against the military. Her own father had proudly served with the U.S. Army in World War I.

But schooling, she had always insisted, was their guaranteed ticket to a better life.

"Nobody can ever take that away from you," Ruth Amanda Davis would often say.

The family was hardly wealthy, but Gordon, Sr. and his wife had always planned to somehow make a way for both their oldest sons to attend college at the same time. There had never been a doubt otherwise.

Granny was deeply concerned that Rodney was making the biggest mistake in his life. She was all too aware of the ongoing Cold War between the U.S. and Soviet Union, and how easily hostilities might have broken out at any moment between the world's two super-powered adversaries. The prospect of her own son possibly being sent off to some far-flung, distant land to someday fight in such a conflict frightened her.

But the shock of Rodney's decision to enlist in the Marine Corps soon wore off, and the entire Davis family soon came to terms with it. As the case with any family, the Davises have endured their share of disagreements and petty squabbles on occasion, but their deep and abiding love for one another has always helped them quickly get over any temporary sour feelings.

Theirs is an admirable quality that is readily apparent to this very day.

With his decision made, the entire family was fully supportive and had rallied around Rodney by the time he was set to leave for South Carolina to begin basic training in early September 1961. He was giddy with anticipation when he reported to the First Recruit Training Battalion, Marine Corps Recruit Depot at Parris Island.

Nestled inside the mouth of the Port Royal Sound in the state's muggy, southern coastal region, Parris Island has always stood as the antithesis of the opulence represented by the nearby Hilton Head Island resort.

Mosquitoes, alligators and sand fleas have long since staked claim to the low-lying area as their own, with the natural swamps and water serving to make only about half of the camp's 8,000-plus acres even habitable for human beings.

Its Spartan physical characteristics and natural isolation are among the reasons why enlisted Marines have trained at Parris Island since 1915. All male recruits from east of the Mississippi River – and all female recruits – report to Parris Island, while male recruits from the west are instead sent to California to attend the Marine Corps Recruit Depot in San Diego.

Not surprisingly, the hardened Parris Island alums are even today just half-joking when they poke fun at their West Coast brethren's relatively easy trek into the Marine brotherhood by calling them "Hollywood" Marines.

More commonly known as "boot camp," U.S. Marine Corps Recruit Training is a grueling 13-week training program that every recruit must complete to become a Marine. During this time, young men and women are tested mentally and physically like never before, broken down as individuals and recast as part of a team of eternal brothers in the U.S. Marine Corps.

It's the one experience every Marine will have shared.

Boot camp equips each Marine with the necessary military fundamentals such as the ability to march in formation, shoot with pinpoint accuracy, defend him or herself with martial arts, survive in deep water, throw hand grenades and quickly don a gas mask in the event of a chemical attack.

In keeping with Marine custom that dictates that every Marine is a rifleman, all recruits must past the standard, two-week rifle qualification course.

Marines typically assert that their recruit training is the most physically and mentally challenging among all the armed forces, often citing a longer, more demanding Physical Fitness Test and the strictest height and weight standards.

The drill instructors who oversee the training are typically fire-breathing staff sergeants or sergeants, boasting anywhere from seven to 10 years of experience. Carefully screened, selected and trained, they are entrusted with the transformation of the raw recruits into bona fide Marines who are knowledgeable and respectful of the Corp's distinctive values, according to the Marine Corps.

Impeccably-dressed with a broad-brimmed campaign hat squarely centered on their close-cropped heads, the D.I.s command immediate attention and even fear at varying levels with their authoritative presence and relentless commands. For some recruits, they are the first strong male figures to enter their lives.

The D.I.s embrace their role, as recruit training is intentionally made stressful as to replicate the pressures and chaos of combat. The young, aspiring Marines learn early on that orders are to be obeyed quickly and that there is no greater sin than to let another Marine down or to leave a fellow Marine on the battlefield.

The moment Davis and the other recruits first arrived on the buses that carried them to their recruit Depot, they were promptly greeted by these hard-nosed drill instructors who quickly brought them up to speed in the proper Marine way of doing things.

"Get off my bus and stand on the yellow footprints now!" they barked at the many shell-shocked recruits like Davis who were now silently questioning their decisions to enlist.

Quickly disembarking from the bus, Davis, like every Marine since him, lined up on the famous "yellow footprints" that was the site of his first formation and where he and the other recruits learned how to correctly stand at attention.

Davis and the other recruits with him that day were then given the opportunity to quickly phone their families to let them know of their safe arrival at Parris Island before receiving all their gear and undergoing the mandated haircuts and medical screenings. They were then effectively cut off entirely from their previous civilian life as they commenced their arduous training regimen on little sleep and food.

An average day for Davis usually began before sunrise, when Reveille was sounded by bugle as a wake-up call for all the recruits to report. Training included a daylong combination of classes, drills or martial arts, and runs until dinner time, which was typically held between 5 and 6 p.m. Recruits were then allotted time to shower, clean their weapons and tidy up their barracks before receiving just an hour of time to engage in personal activities such as preparing uniforms or equipment, writing letters, working out or doing laundry.

Lights-out was strictly enforced at 10 p.m.

Like those who both preceded him and later followed, Davis and the new recruits with him quickly deduced upon their arrival at Parris Island that it was best to be as next to invisible as possible so as to avoid the wrath of a D.I. There is no worse nightmare for any recruit than to be singled out by a drill instructor for a mistake. The D.I.s often like to refer to their harsh methods as "proper guidance," but such mental lashings are unsettling to say the least.

Davis was determined to do his best to avoid that scenario as much as possible, so he did his best to make sure he always did things the right way at all times.

The Marine way.

Like so many recruits, the sudden drastic change in lifestyle initially proved a difficult initial adjustment for Davis. He wasn't used to strange people jumping in his face and barking orders at him, and struggled initially in the transition to the more regimented way of life and strict discipline always expected of Marines. He quickly became homesick in his first extended stay away from his family.

"My dearest mother," he wrote in letter dated Sept. 28, 1961.

"I received your letter and was glad to hear from you. I'm trying very hard not to get in trouble any more so I can make it back home for Christmas. I will be just on time if I can make it out with this platoon. And I miss you so I can explain it. Some nights I lie in the bed and cry and wish I was home with you.

I like it in this platoon. The D.I. [Drill Instructor] is hard, but I am used to it now and it's a lot easier to handle. At first when they would holler at me, I would get mad. But now I know he is just doing his job and I'm a big guy and they want me to be a leader and are hard on me."

It wasn't easy, but Davis persevered, writing home when he could find the time and detailing his many grueling days, lengthy training exercises and constant feelings of exhaustion.

But he was never the type to sit and wallow in self-pity or doubt about his situation. He had never done as much while growing up through the many trials and tribulations that came with living under Jim Crow.

So he wasn't about to start then. Not when he was so tantalizingly close to realizing a dream and becoming a U.S. Marine.

Giving up was never an option.

"He understood that he had to work harder and be better than his white colleagues," Gordon Davis said of his brother.

The timeless beauty of Marine boot camp is that it serves to make every recruit – male or female - come face-to-face with his or her own deepest fears and weaknesses and to devise clever ways to overcome them.

Always physically strong and daring, Davis' lone Achilles' heel of sorts had always been in the water, as he'd never been a particularly good swimmer. His siblings used to laugh when their much taller brother would stray further out in the water than they could manage and pretend to be going through the motions of swim strokes, all the while standing upright on his feet.

In fact, Davis had briefly even toyed with following in his father's footsteps and joining the Navy while growing up, but quickly had a change of heart after realizing how much more swimming would be required in that particular branch of the military.

But there was no escaping it in the Marine Corps either, so Davis was suddenly faced with having to overcome that long-dreaded obstacle about a month into boot camp as part of the swimming and water survival portion of the training regimen. At boot camp, recruits wearing backpacks, helmets, flak jackets and rifles are required to leap into the water from a tower and "swim" on their back, using their packs as flotation devices. The goal of the exercise is to teach the recruits how to survive in water, retain their equipment, stand ready to help others and to continue the mission.

Theirs is an amphibious service, so water survival training for Marines is necessary to increase their competence and chances of survival in an amphibious environment. Failure to pass this part of the training program results in a recruit being dropped to a different company to restart training and attempt to qualify again.

Should a recruit fail twice, he or she will be evaluated to see if a third opportunity is warranted. If not, the recruit can be administratively separated from service and sent home.

Davis struggled initially, failing the swimming test on his first try.

"You know what happens to me [in the water]," he nonchalantly wrote his brother Howard shortly afterwards. "I like to have drowned. The drill instructor threw me in and I swam about 75 feet in water, and I swam to the side, but you have to swim about 100 yards before you pass, so I have to go back for lessons."

Davis was reassigned to another company, but he was determined that his lack of great proficiency in the water wasn't going to prevent him from being a Marine. He set his mind to that goal and soon made the most of his additional lessons to quickly improve enough to easily pass the second time around.

His biggest hurdle cleared, Davis went on to especially excel during the regimen's two-week focus on marksmanship, and proudly graduated from boot camp in December 1961. Like all those before him who had completed Recruit Training, Davis received the coveted Eagle, Globe and Anchor emblem that have been a part of the Marine uniform since 1868 and the Corp's official symbol since 1955.

The Eagle with spread wings represented the proud nation Davis so dearly loved, while the globe and anchor pointed to the U.S. Marines' worldwide presence and naval tradition, respectively.

Friends and family immediately noticed the difference from the somewhat unsure young man who had left home for the first time just a few months earlier. He was now a proud man of the world, cocksure of himself after enduring 13 taxing weeks of boot camp hell and living to tell about it.

Davis was now officially a U.S. Marine, and had begun carrying himself with the unmistakable air of confidence, discipline and distinctive sense of deliberateness that came with that title.

Private Rodney M. Davis was then transferred to Marine Corps Base, Camp Lejeune, where he would undergo Individual Combat Training with the Second Battalion, First Infantry Training Regiment, graduating in February 1962.

****

The U.S. military had long been at the cutting edge when it came to making significant headway in race relations. President Harry S. Truman's decision on July 26, 1948 to order the integration of the nation's armed forces was initially met with bitter resistance, particularly from disgruntled Southern politicians who would later abandon the Democratic Party and become "Dixiecrats."

Executive Order 9981 was unprecedented in that it intimated that "separate was not equal" roughly six years before the Supreme Court formally declared as much with its landmark Brown vs. Board of Education decision in 1954.

Even changes in the military, however, were still slow in coming, but finally came to fruition out of necessity following the outbreak of the Korean War in 1950. By the end of that conflict three years later, the last of the military's segregated units had been dissolved and the momentum for equality and civil rights had begun carrying over into American society as a whole.

The armed forces, however, still only mirrored the rest of the country and had its own heated racial issues with which it had to contend.

African-Americans have fought in all of America's wars, but have at times faced as much hostility or more from their fellow countrymen who were white as they did from the enemy.

Davis had discovered as much first-hand shortly after initially enlisting in the Marines. In a letter written to one of his brothers shortly after his arrival on Parris Island for basic training, he wrote of the problems he and other African-American Marines were having with some of their white drill instructors.

Davis said he and other black Marines were "called nigger and animals. We are the lowest thing on earth to them, and they can talk about you anyway they want to, and you can't even bat an eye or you're wrong."

In another letter, Davis recounted a fight between him and a racist white Marine who had called him several derogatory names before spitting on his freshly-shined boots. Davis appeared to have derived special pride in easily beating down the racist Marine twice that day as retribution.

First in their subsequent exchange of blows when the incident initially took place. And again later after a platoon sergeant caught the two fighting and ordered them to instead settle their differences in the boxing ring.

"I'm behaving other than that," Davis wrote home.

In another undated letter sent home to his mother from Camp Lejeune prior to his deployment overseas, Davis wrote of being in formation one day when a white drill instructor ordered their entire company of 260 men to beat down a lone African-American Marine from another company who just happened to be strolling through their designated area.

Davis joined several others in disobeying the order and instead fighting a group of white men from his own unit. For defending a fellow African-American Marine, Davis said he had been ordered to appear before his company commander. It is unclear if he received punishment of any sort for his role in the racially-charged incident. There were no such indications in his official military records.

"The guy got his leg broke," Davis later wrote home. "I've got to go get antiseptic to put on my scratches. I enjoyed the fight, but it really hurt my feelings to see all those crackers jump on that dude.

"These people are crazy, all of them."

But his deep love of country wouldn't allow him to ever become bitter, no matter the shameful treatment afforded him by his own countrymen. Davis' affinity for America grew even as Cold War tensions rose and the threat of a possible shooting war with the Soviet Union appeared more and more likely with the advent of the Cuban Missile Crisis in October 1962.

"Dear Mother," he wrote in a letter home dated Oct. 29, 1962.

"Just a few lines to let you know I received your letter and was glad to always hear from you. I write this letter at Camp Lejeune, where I arrived at about 4 o'clock today. I don't know what I will be doing since I have been separated from my unit. I could say I am glad because I would miss the war if we have one. But I kind of want to be with the boys if we have to fight, then go to a new unit. But all I can do is wait and see what happens. Hope you and the family are doing fine.

Tell them I said hello.

Love always,

Rod"

But the quickly escalating crisis over Cuba would soon pass, and a direct confrontation with the world's only other superpower at the time was just barely averted.

But Davis no doubt noted the irony of the situation in which suddenly found himself.

Like many of his former classmates who went on to attend HBCUs following high school, many in Atlanta at either Morehouse or Spelman, he, too, was preparing for war. Only this one of a different sort. Davis was training for a hot shooting war overseas in which he would be asked to defend the liberties he himself couldn't enjoy at home.

His old friends were also preparing to wage a campaign for their own freedoms, but it would be one without the same grand scale of ugly violence, and it would take place at home on American soil.

After finishing Individual Combat Training, Davis remained at Camp Lejeune after joining Company "K", Third Battalion, Second Marines, Second Marine Division, FMF, and serving there as a rifleman until May 1964. An excellent shot and a disciplined Marine, he thrived in his new post. Davis was promoted to Private First Class on April 1, 1962 and later to Lance Corporal on Jan. 1, 1964.

Davis continued to advance his career by enrolling in a number of specialized correspondence courses such as Tactics of The Marine Rifle Squad (1963), The Marine Non-Commissioned Officer (1964), Military Functions in Civil Disturbances and Disasters (1964), Map and Aerial Photo Reading (1964), Operations against Guerrilla Forces (1965) and M60 Machine Gun Schools (1966). Each of the Washington, D.C.-based Marine Corps Institute classes were considered non-resident professional military education.

He was now busy at all times and quickly becoming a man of the world, but Rodney Davis' heart clearly remained home in Macon with his family.

"Mother, you may think that I'm a very wrong person because I don't write," he wrote in a letter penned on July 10, 1963, "but I try all the time and all of them end up saying nothing, so I don't mail them. And I want you to know I don't ever go through a day without thinking about you and how much I miss home!"

****

Rodney Davis was now a proud U.S. Marine who was about to embark on the biggest adventure of his life to herald the completion of his transformation into a man. But a quick trip home on his final leave before heading oversees for the first time was proof enough that the household rules his parents had set for their children never changed even if he did.

It was an early Sunday morning and the Davis family was preparing to attend Sunday school just as they had always done every week. Because there was one just bathroom in a house filled with so many people, both Gordon Davis, Sr. and his wife were adamant that their children were to exclusively focus on getting up, cleaning their rooms, eating breakfast and taking turns in the shower so that the family would always be on time.

Their parents were adamant that there was to be no playing whatsoever or even reading of the newspaper until after the family had returned home from church. Giving proper thanks to the Lord each Sunday superseded any ancillary plans. The whole family was expected to be ready to go the moment Gordon Davis, Sr. was dressed and ready.

It was early September 1963 when Rodney made his way back home for the first time in a lengthy period of time. Looking sharp in his neatly-creased Marine dress uniform, he coolly sat down in the living room and grabbed the Sunday newspaper off the table where it had been sitting after being picked up out of the driveway.

Then just eight years old, his younger sister Debra was the first of his younger siblings to enter the living room after getting herself ready. She was stunned to see her brother reading the paper when he knew they weren't allowed to do so just yet.

Rodney, who was then 21 years old, just figured the rules no longer applied to him. He was now a U.S. Marine after all, getting ready to head overseas on behalf of his country. He figured that meant that he was a man now free to do whatever he pleased, wherever he pleased. His parents' home included.

"Awww, you're gonna get in trouble," Debra warned her older brother. "You just wait until or Momma or Daddy sees you."

"It's no big deal," Rodney told his sister. "Everybody reads the paper."

It was moments later that Granny walked into the living room and immediately snatched the paper from her unsuspecting son's hands as he was reading it. An irate Rodney instinctively jumped up, only to be dressed down by his mother in the presence of not only his siblings, but also a college friend of Gordon's who had come home with him for the weekend from Fort Valley State.

"What's the matter with you?" Ruth Amanda Davis asked her son. "You know we don't do that! Now bend down so I can pull your ear."

Pulling their ears was Granny's more preferred way of disciplining her children when the situation called for it. And she knew how to do it in such a manner so that it hurt enough that her kids quickly deduced that it was a punishment to be avoided. Rodney was now a fighting man in the U.S. Marine Corps, but he knew there was never any disobeying his mother. Not only did he respect her too much to ever do so, but there was no question that his father would have come down hard on him if ever did so.

Gordon Davis, Sr. was the unquestioned ruler of the Davis home and his rules were non-negotiable.

"Okay," Rodney allowed, bending all the way down to allow his much-shorter mother complete access to his ears. He took his punishment and then began crying as he slipped back into the same chair in which he had just been enjoying the newspaper only a few minutes earlier.

"I just saw a U.S. Marine back down," Gordon's friend joked later with Rodney about the incident.

"I didn't back down," Rodney retorted, trying to save face the best he could, "but I'm not gonna ever hit or disrespect my mother."

The lesson Rodney took with him back to Camp Lejeune from that day on was clear. The sight of a towering U.S. Marine may have been among the most recognizable symbols of American military power and a source of great trepidation for the nation's adversaries from around the globe, but not in the Davis household.

He would always be Rodney to his parents and show them the respect they deserved by adhering to the rules of their house.

****

On September 21, 1963, the Marines of K Company boarded the transport ship USS Sandoval in Morehead City, N.C. before sailing off to take part in an amphibious training cruise throughout the Mediterranean.

The life-altering five-month cruise included memorable stops in Spain, Sardinia, Sicily, Italy, France, Greece and Cyprus.

They were picturesque cities all, beautiful ports previously unknown to Davis other than in the alluring pictures in books he read while growing up. Scenic venues that were equally as charming as they were historic in venerable locales like Rome and other hot spots throughout Italy and in Spain.

Still, Davis sounded lonely at times, always longing for his beloved family and for the familiar confines of Macon. As much became obvious in a series of letters he wrote while at sea.

"Dear Mother," he wrote in one dispatch, dated Oct. 29, 1963.

I trust that you are in the best of health at the reading of this letter. I promised to write, so I decided to keep my promise for a change and write more often.

I guess you can say I am doing "OK." I have [guard] duty tonight, so I am writing this letter from a lonely room, sitting and looking at the lights over Naples, Italy while all my boys are on liberty and having fun.

This is the third foreign port we have been to, and, at the first two, I did get to see most of the historical spots and landmarks. But I am going to Rome tomorrow for a three-day tour.

Mother, tell Daddy I say hello and my brothers and sister. I wrote Gordon the last time I wrote you. Mother, I will close with these words, 'I love you and always will.'

Your son,

Rodney"

Davis was again pulling a lonely guard duty shift about two months later on Christmas Night, 1963, when he penned what he called "the hardest letter I ever tried to write." Christmas was always a special time for the entire Davis family, as they always gathered in Macon to celebrate the birth of Jesus in one another's company.

He couldn't help but think of his family at that time of year and longed to again be with them.

"I hope you and the family enjoy your X-Mas holiday and I am wishing you a Happy New Year," he wrote.

I would have written sooner, but the last mail that went off the ship was on the 9th of December, and I don't think that it is going out again to the 29th, so it was no need to write. I could have written sooner, so I have no excuse.

Mother, this is the worst X-Mas I have ever spent, and I really miss home. I still can't find anything to write about. Tell Daddy I say 'Hi' and my bros and sis. I am writing Gordon today also.

Your son,

Rodney"

That forgettable holiday experience notwithstanding, his first experience overseas left an indelible mark on Davis like nothing before in that it opened his eyes to the rest of the large and very different world waiting out there to be seen and experienced. It was an epiphany that likely played a key role in his subsequent decision to seek a prestigious embassy security detail posting in London or Japan the following year.

Serving on the security detail at the U.S. Embassy in London, England – the pristine capital of America's staunchest and most revered ally - is considered perhaps one of the most prestigious posts in the entire Marine Corps.

Not to mention one of the most luxurious as well. Yet Davis had fretted about his chances in landing such a sought-after posting.

"I hope I can get one of them," he wrote in a letter to his mother dated May 13, 1964. "... I have already been turned down once, so I'm not getting my hopes up. This and getting promotions have a lot to do with what I do in the future. If I don't get one of them, goodbye to the Marine Corps. I am getting to be a short-timer, you know. This time next year, I will be out."

Many career Marines had longed for such an exalted assignment, making the competition intense for the few 65 or so spots available. All those vying for the post underwent the additional intensive background screening necessary for the high-level security clearance needed.

Davis' fears about not being selected proved unfounded as he was indeed among the small number tapped for duty in London starting on June 15, 1964 with a three-year stint with the U.S. Marine Detachment, Naval Activities.

He quickly found life to be very good in the historic English capital, both personally and professionally.

Davis immediately took to his new staggered duty schedule that usually called for four-hour security shifts, followed by eight hours of free time before four more hours of duty. As the armed gatekeepers to the official U.S representatives in a foreign land, the Marines dutifully stood post at five different locations in and around the embassy. The admiral's entrance to the side of the embassy was where haughty dignitaries such as high-ranking public officials, celebrities and the like would enter the compound. It was, understandably, the one spot most preferred by the young, star-crossed Marines, many of whom were now overseas for the first time in their lives.

The front post was the least-liked of them all, as those who drew duty there were forced to mostly stand still for long periods of time while dutifully checking the identification of those seeking entry into the embassy. Other guard stations included one at the front desk, a 2nd-floor post and a roving patrol around the embassy premises.

Known for his quiet, but friendly demeanor, Davis quickly took to his new duties, and earned repeated assignments to watch the coveted admiral's entrance.

It wasn't surprising to those who served with him in London because they recalled Davis as "the consummate Marine."

"He never drew attention to himself, but he was always where he needed to be and doing what he needed to do," recalled Robert "Bob" Schlafke, a retired Fort Lauderdale, Florida police detective who served in London with Davis for roughly a year. "I just know when something needed to be done, he was there."

Davis' superiors in London were likewise impressed with his performance. Major N.A. Nelson, who commanded the Marine detachment, gave Davis excellent marks and lauded him for his overall professionalism in several fitness reports found in Davis' official military records.

"Sgt. Davis is a quiet, highly reliable and efficient NCO," Nelson wrote in one report dated June 20, 1967. "Because of his quiet manner, Sgt. Davis does not make a strong first impression. However, his steady performance and the way he completes his assignments make a lasting impression."

In a later report, Nelson described Davis as "reliable, trustworthy and conscientious in the performance of his duties.

His potential is excellent and, with experience, will develop into a fine NCO.''

Nelson cited Davis for excellence in both endurance and personal appearance and gave him above-average marks for his strong military presence, attention to duty and leadership skills among other things. Yet, in perhaps the greatest irony of all, Nelson famously noted in two different evaluations of Davis that he'd seen nothing to judge Davis' ability to think and act promptly in an unexpected manner or while under great stress.

He would later hear otherwise.

But Davis' tour of duty in London wasn't entirely free of some minor problems, however. Perhaps it was his strong sense of right and wrong that was behind his reprimand on March 25, 1966 for disrespectful language towards a superior non-commissioned officer and his restriction to base for two weeks. Davis did not appeal the punishment and learned his lesson from the matter.

He was a Marine, and that meant always acting like one at all times. Even around those he didn't particularly like or respect all that much.

But the incident was quickly forgotten as Davis thrived in his new environment.

Unlike most other posts around the world, the U.S. Marines in London enjoyed the enviable perks that came with living in a posh barracks that was conveniently located in the middle of one of London's trendiest and most exclusive neighborhoods.

The facility was a far cry from other mostly dull or sometimes even shoddy Marine barracks posts throughout the world, most of which were intentionally designed with the purpose of separating the Marines from the civilian population while reinforcing discipline and training, and furthering an esprit de corps.

Their four-story housing facility at St. John's Wood in London offered a little bit of everything to the young Marines always in search of something close by to occupy their time while idling in between their guard shifts. The relatively ritzy accommodations upstairs included a cavernous gym that came with a full-sized basketball court, office space and an equipment room. Among the basement's many features were a cozy lounge where the young Marines might relax in their off time, an indoor firing range, an armory, a dining hall and a full-service recreation room complete with a television set, a dartboard and ping-pong tables.

Davis was thrilled with his new surroundings, but his thoughts never strayed far from his family back in Macon. It was around Thanksgiving 1964 when he first got word that his younger brother Howard had accidentally shot himself in the leg when a gun round had inadvertently went off and caromed off the ground into his leg.

Howard Davis was OK, but his big brother had to make sure.

"I am living like a king," he wrote his brother Howard in letter dated November 29, 1964, *"and I've got to stop it, so I'm giving it [$60] to you. Take the money and get my sis and little brother something for Christmas. I would have sent them more because I am saving about a hundred dollars a month, which I just started about two months ago, but I don't want to draw anything out yet. I am also writing Mom and Gordon today. Don't you go and get shot again before I see you. Be cool until I see you.*

Your Bro,

Rodney"

Family would always come first for Davis, but his fellow Marines had quickly become his new extended kinfolk.

Harold McConnell served in London with Davis for about 18 months, in which time the two men quickly came to be close friends. The two Marines often spoke of their vastly different upbringings in their free time, usually over drinks and in between games of darts at the local pub across the street.

McConnell would often joke with Davis about the slow delivery in his speech and very pronounced deep Southern twang, nicknaming him "Duck" as to make his point.

"I'd never heard anybody talk like him," McDonnell laughs now.

Davis would rib McConnell back in kind about his own upbringing in his native Idaho, but the two men's shared love of country, sense of duty and pride in being a Marine easily outweighed all their differences.

"Rodney was always great to be around," McConnell said. "He had a helluva personality and he was very charismatic. You just enjoyed being around him."

The two men never once over their many talks discussed the issue of race, or any of the tumultuous happenings back at home in the United States. Both men likely knew the reality of it all to be an uncomfortable truth best not verbalized.

But his presence overseas in London and elsewhere never precluded Davis from knowing of all the turmoil that was taking place back in the United States, particularly in his hometown of Macon and elsewhere where his family members were.

There was no escaping the constant media coverage of all the stiff resistance the Civil Rights Movement was facing in the South – including the mind-numbing violence - in just about every newspaper, magazine or television program. He gathered even more information upon his weekly phone calls home to Macon.

Not that Davis needed any reminding of racism. He often spoke to his brothers of encountering intolerance overseas as well, mostly in the form of preconceived racial stereotypes. Perhaps only because they were U.S. servicemen, African-American soldiers were not physically run out of establishments in Europe as was often the case in Macon and other parts of the South. But they were hardly welcomed with open arms either, Davis often reported home.

Intolerance knew no boundaries.

Yet his family back in Macon always did their best to assure him they were OK, even as some of the most trying times in American history raged around them.

"He knew how it was when he left here and nothing had changed," Howard Davis said. "He knew we were in good hands and were taking care of ourselves. We were more concerned about his being away from home."

Yet it's easy to wonder whether Davis ever managed to reconcile the paradox he appeared to have felt of the very snug life he was enjoying at the time in London with his profound remorse about the tense social climate he must have known his beloved family was simultaneously enduring with the deteriorating state of race relations back in his native Georgia.

Maybe because he wasn't there to help shield them as he'd previously done.

"Dear Mother," he wrote in a letter written sometime in the summer of 1964.

"I received your letter and was glad as always to hear from you, and know the family is well and getting along OK.

As far as me, I guess I'm OK. I really am sorry about not writing. I don't know what is wrong with me, Mother. I think I am crazy or something at times. You are the best mother and my Daddy is the best man I've ever met in my life, so if I'm just a no-good person, it's nothing you or him have done. I think at times you and he have been too good to me, and I don't know how to accept people being nice to me. I have to find out since I have been living with other people who always hurt the people that are nice to them. I don't know why I would want to hurt you and [his father]. Momma, I love you and always will. Don't give up on me yet. (smile). I'm staying here and when I play some [basketball], I'm trying not to feel so bad about what I've done. I am sorry and I won't let it happen again. I know you're saying 'I've heard that before', but this time I mean it.

I have a lot of things I wish I could talk with you about. I may be getting married soon, but I don't know how to write you about her. I have already extended for another year in the Corps, so it will be June 1966 before I get home again. I hope it's for good. I am going to try and write you and tell you about [Judy] in my next letter.

Tell my Daddy I said hello and my bros and sis. I am writing Howard and Gordon today also."

Davis' engaging personality had won people over throughout his entire life and his arrival in London had brought only more of the same. It had been very shortly after his arrival in country that Davis first met the woman to whom he had been referring, the one who would be his future wife. A native of Barbados, the beautiful Judy Humphrey had been working as a secretary at a nearby embassy when she first met the tall American in the suave Marine dress blue uniform.

Somewhat tall herself for a woman at 5-9 ½, she was a few months shy of her 20th birthday when she first met the man who would forever hold her heart.

Davis had been smitten immediately after first spotting her walking alone in a park near the U.S. Embassy. He soon saw his future bride in the park again, only this time accompanied by the serious boyfriend she had at the time.

Undeterred, Davis went up and introduced himself anyway.

Judy, however, didn't know what to think at first, unsure as to what to make of what she perceived as the somewhat contradictory sides of Davis' personality. He would at times showcase the same brash determination that was evident in their first acquaintance, but yet also displayed a natural quiet disposition during others. Unsure what to make of this handsome U.S. Marine, she admitted to wondering early on whether his quiet side was some sort of twisted American arrogance. But the two quickly got to know one another and fell deeply in love.

The couple soon married and later welcomed their daughters, Nicky and Samantha, on August 21, 1965 and July 21, 1966, respectively.

Just like his decision to enlist in the Marines a few years earlier, Rodney had made the decision to marry first and only let others in his family know of his decision after the fact. But it was the first major one he'd ever made in his life without at least first consulting his older brother. In fact, he didn't even call Gordon from London with the news until the day before his wedding.

"I'm gonna marry her," Rodney Davis informed his older brother. "What do you think about that?"

Gordon Davis admitted to being a little surprised by the news, but his love and support for his brother had always been unwavering. He had his back no matter what, and that unquestioned loyalty had always gone both ways.

"If that's what you want to do, that's great!" Gordon Davis replied, his only regret being that he could not somehow make it to London by the next day to personally witness his little brother's nuptials.

"You know I'll always support you no matter what you ever do."

Like all Marines serving overseas, Davis needed command approval before marrying a foreign national. His superiors quickly approved the union, thereby cancelling the permanent change of station orders he had previously received that would have sent him to the U.S. Marine Corps Air Station in Cherry Point, N.C. by June 1966.

Now a happily married family man, Davis continued to thrive personally and professionally as well. He was promoted to corporal on Jan. 1, 1966, and soon received another elevation in rank to sergeant on Dec. 1, 1966.

Satisfied with both his personal and professional life, Davis had first extended his tenure in the Marine Corps for a year on August 30, 1965 before signing on for six more years as of August 31, 1966.

Vietnam beckoned.

CHAPTER 7

COMING HOME AND FACING THE WAR

It was the middle of June 1967, and the mood was especially jubilant that one special summer afternoon as the entire Davis family gathered in the backyard of the family residence at 2154 Neal Avenue in giddy anticipation of Rodney Davis' return home before his deployment to Vietnam.

Unsure as to when exactly his airplane would be landing in Atlanta that day, the proud Davis clan was already assembled and eager to greet him. They frolicked outdoors in the backyard for most of the warm, sunny afternoon, joking amongst themselves that each plane passing overhead en route to the Atlanta airport might be the one with Rodney aboard.

"Maybe that's him!" anxious family members would offer amongst themselves as they bided their time.

He was supposed to call upon landing, so that family members could immediately begin the 80-mile or so trek to the airport to pick him up and bring him home.

Rodney had managed to make it back home a few times per year as part of the 30 days of annual leave Marines were allotted, but this occasion promised to be even considerably more momentous than before.

Not only was the entire Davis family ready to proudly send off one of their own to the growing conflict in southeast Asia, but they were all equally as excited to warmly greet Rodney's new family for the first time.

The family had been given a few months in advance to prepare for his impending departure to the war in Vietnam, but the grim reality of where he was soon headed was only now hitting home. It had been several months since Rodney had initially informed his family during his last trip back to Macon during the fall of 1966 that he planned to request duty in Vietnam once his three-year stint in London at the U.S. Embassy concluded in May.

Rodney Davis had driven to Albany, Georgia shortly after arriving back home to personally inform his older brother of his decision.

"It's time to stop being a 'show' Marine and time to be a 'real' Marine," he explained to Gordon. "Nobody is more qualified for this than I am."

"You do what you have to do," his older brother replied. "You know I'll always have your back no matter what."

Rodney had also made Gordon aware of his intentions to send his young family back to Macon while he was away at war, and sought a promise from his older sibling that he would always look after Nicky and Samantha in the event something should happen to him.

Knowing all too well there was no changing his brother's mind once he'd made a decision, Gordon could only readily support Rodney's decision. So he gladly agreed to look out after his brother's young family while he was away and beyond in the event he were to die in Vietnam.

"He wanted me to raise them as Davises," Gordon Davis said.

Most men might have understandably struggled with the decision to voluntarily leave a young wife and two infant children behind to go fight a war, but Rodney was not like most men and came to his decision rather easily.

He felt his entire life had been leading up to that very moment, harking back to his childhood days of dreaming of being a U.S. Marine and fighting for his country.

It's what he knew he was meant to do.

Davis had been driven and single-minded in purpose during his intense training over the years for that inevitable mission, and felt it was his destiny beckoning at that time. Not to mention his duty. He truly believed that to eschew his calling was to not be true to himself. The decision was easier to make because he knew his family would be well taken care of in his absence.

As you might imagine, Judy Davis wasn't exactly thrilled initially with her husband's decision, but she knew that's what he had his heart set on doing.

"He realized there was a war going on, and that was his duty and his job," Gordon Davis explained. "He didn't bullshit and scratch his head like most people would have. That's what he had prepared himself for his entire life. He wanted to be a Marine and do that. He wanted to do something he thought he was the best prepared for in the world to do.

"It wasn't a matter of how [Judy] felt or how anybody else felt. It was his time and his place, and he was going to do that."

So the decision was made, and Judy and the girls would go to Macon in his absence.

His new wife had a few relatives in London, but Rodney had insisted his own large and very close-knit family in Macon would best look after them all while he was serving in Vietnam. Judy soon agreed that she and the couple's two small children would at least initially move into the Davis family home on Neal Avenue with Rodney's mother, father and young siblings while he was away at war.

"I knew that going to Vietnam was something he wanted to do," she was quoted as saying in 1987 following the commissioning of the ship named in her late husband's honor. "He was a military man, and that was his career."

"He was willing and ready to go to Vietnam because he felt he was doing a service," Ruth Amanda Davis said of her son during the same interview with the Macon Courier. "He didn't hesitate about going."

The two most prominent women in his life also knew Rodney wouldn't have been happy enjoying the comforts of London while other Marines were doing the fighting and dying thousands of miles away in Vietnam.

He was certain that he was also supposed to be there.

But Rodney Davis was first excited about again enjoying the simple comforts of home again before shipping out, all the more so because this leave was for a whole month rather than the previous 10-day stints that had all sailed by way too quickly. His many letters home over the previous six years show him to have been very family-oriented and particularly close to both his parents and his older brother. He had written as often as possible in the years since he'd joined the Marines and had even sent money home to his siblings on a number of occasions.

Rodney's correspondence over the years had made it very clear that he had always felt very guilty about his military duties keeping him away from his family in Macon for such lengthy periods, often sounding very lonely as a result.

"Mother, I love you more than anyone in this whole world," he wrote in one undated letter, "and find it hard to be miles away from a person that you love."

While away, Rodney often expressed his great regret for not writing home even more. His letters home were never all that long, but he was always comfortable in expressing how he was feeling to those he loved most in the world.

Davis had never been one for long, bloated prose, as his writing style mirrored his own simple, down-to-earth personality. He asked pointed questions about the well-being of all of his family members – but especially his siblings - in every letter home to his parents.

Yet, he proved as direct in his writing as he had always been in his conversations with people, never sugar-coating things.

Not even when it came to himself.

"Mother, you may think that I am a very, very wrong person because I don't write," he penned in one letter dated July 10, 1963, "but I try all the time and all of them end up saying nothing, so I don't mail them. And I want you to know I don't ever go through a whole day without thinking about you and how much I miss home."

The Davis family had always done just about everything together while he was growing up, including eating dinner with one another every night courtesy of a rigid house rule that mandated that everybody be home by 5:30 p.m.

There were many times when the Davis children didn't understand why their parents insisted on doing what they did, although they do now. They formed lifelong bonds during the course of those many shared meals and memorable conversations, and the kind of deep affinity for one another that would last the rest of their lives.

They were family, and always would be. No matter any circumstances.

So suddenly being thrust in a whole new world so far removed from his loved ones wasn't always easy for Rodney. He struggled initially with feelings of loneliness his first few years in the Marines, but he persevered.

So maybe that giddy anticipation and palpable excitement he felt about finally getting back to his roots in Macon for the first lengthy time in a while was why he never called after safely landing in Atlanta with his new family.

Family members were still outside awaiting word from him when a strange taxi suddenly pulled up, finally coming to a complete stop in front of the house at 2154 Neal Avenue early on a warm weekday afternoon.

They were all unsure what to think at first, but quickly caught on when a tall, lanky figure in civilian clothes began making his way out of the vehicle.

"Look, it's Rodney!" somebody yelled.

Rodney Davis was home at last, and he had brought his new family with him for all to see. The larger-than-life smile that suddenly appeared on Rodney's face and the sight of so many Davis family members immediately dropping what they were doing and flocking out into the street to warmly greet him spoke to the deep love they shared for one another.

His relatively short time home were giddy days, but very busy ones, too, as Rodney Davis did the best he could during the near month he was home to make up for precious lost time with his beloved parents, as well as his four siblings and his many close friends. He loved them all dearly and relished the opportunity to be back among them again and in familiar surroundings. There was also the not-so-small matter of making sure his young family was becoming acclimated to the new and vastly different environment in Macon that would be their home for the foreseeable future.

Gordon Davis Sr. had wasted no time in beginning preparations the minute he received word that his second-oldest child would be coming home, bringing his new daughter-in-law and grandchildren to Macon along with him. In addition to making the rounds at the local stores with his wife to grab up as many toys as he could for his first two baby grandchildren he intended on showering with love, he got right to work in fixing up the upstairs room in the house that was being shared at the time by young Howard, Robert and Debra.

It wasn't easy, but he was thrilled to add a new air condition unit upstairs, take up the old carpet and replace it with a new one and fix anything else that required his attention. Gordon Davis, Sr. was determined that his son and young family would essentially have a comfortable suite of their own during what would ultimately be Rodney's last visit home.

Rodney's displaced siblings were only happy to make do with their alternate sleeping arrangements for their brother's new family.

For her part, Ruth Amanda Davis had something particular in mind to welcome her son back home after such a lengthy absence.

Namely ice cream.

As a child, Rodney's penchant for it had quickly become the stuff of legends. He could eat ice cream anytime, anyplace. The flavor usually didn't matter.

His mother wanted to make her son's long-anticipated return home before going to Vietnam all the more pleasurable, so Ruth Amanda Davis had diligently put aside enough money over the course of several weeks to go and load up on 31 different flavors of Baskin Robbins ice cream as a special homecoming treat.

It hadn't been an easy task in gathering so much ice cream in the house while somehow managing to keep young Debra and

Robert from helping themselves to it, but the determined family matriarch had managed. She wanted everything about Rodney's return home to be perfect.

But Rodney had changed in the roughly six years since he had first left Macon. He was no longer the unsure young man who was just coming into his own, a guy who had initially been so homesick during boot camp that he had cried himself to sleep on more than one occasion.

"Are you sure you don't want any ice cream, Rodney?" his mother asked. "It's always been your favorite."

"Nah, not right now, Mom," he answered back. "Just don't really feel like it today. Maybe a little later though. Go ahead and give some to Debra and Robert. I'm sure they've been wanting some for a while now anyway."

Rodney Davis was now a man, a proud U.S. Marine with a young family to look after as he prepared to go off to war. Not all the things that had once so easily tickled his fancy in childhood would further apply.

As such, Rodney no longer constantly yearned for the taste of ice cream like he once did, and he barely touched the bevy of it his mother had brought home. His opportunistic younger siblings, however, wasted no time in digging in.

Ruth Amanda Davis was no doubt torn with mixed emotions about this latest development. On one hand, she was likely a little sad because it was no clear like never before that he was no longer the little boy whose eyes instantly lit up at the very mention of ice cream. But she was probably also just as equally proud of the fine man and doting husband and father he'd become while he had been away serving his country.

But she was mother, and would always love him and worry about him just the same.

For much of his all-too-brief final stay at home, the specter of Vietnam was the ugly, 500-pound gorilla in the room nobody really wanted to acknowledge. There had been some small talk on occasion from family and friends imploring Rodney to stay safe and keep his head down while there, but everybody had mostly skirted around the issue. Nobody wanted to be the one to first seriously broach the very sensitive subject. The Davis family knew all too well that Rodney's next tour of duty would be an extremely dangerous one, and that young Americans were dying in the unpopular war in alarming numbers by that time.

Nobody dared think the unthinkable.

"To him, it was like your getting a driver's license," Gordon Davis said. "He was going to work. It was going to work to him. You go to work and figure nothing is going to happen to you. To him, he was going to work and it was nothing to be excited about.

"He just happened to work at where they shot at you."

But serious talk of the war did come up during at least one unforgettable dinner conversation between Rodney and several close friends and family members just prior to his departure. Rodney had done his best to allay all their concerns during his time back in Macon because he had to know they were going to be OK. The last thing any service member headed off to war needs is to be worried about what's happening "back in the world" and have his mind focused back there or on anything else other than ensuring his own survival.

A distracted Marine will soon be a dead Marine.

However, George Shorter, one of his closest friends, finally mustered the courage to give voice to the one overriding concern the entire Davis family and their many friends had all shared, but dared not express. A soldier in the U.S. Army, Shorter just happened to be home on leave himself from Vietnam when he stopped by to see his longtime pal for the first time in a while and to let him know what to expect when he soon arrived in country.

Shorter was very candid in warning Rodney Davis to always take care of himself first, and to be sure to bring himself back home to those who loved him.

"Don't be a hero," Shorter advised his friend.

Rodney Davis suddenly turned serious, looking his worried friend directly in the eye.

"That might be what the Army does," he assured him with his trademark matter-of-fact bluntness, "but that's not what Marines do. I'm going to do my job over there. If that means being a hero, I'll be a hero. I'm just going to do my job."

Davis reported to Marine Corps Base, Camp Pendleton in California on July 11, 1967 to begin preparations to go to Vietnam.

CHAPTER 8
VIETNAM AND OPERATION SWIFT

Davis had foregone a relatively cushy, yet extremely prestigious tour of duty as part of the security detail at the U.S. Embassy in London when he volunteered for service in Southeast Asia. He first arrived in the Republic of Vietnam on Aug. 14, 1967 when his plane landed in Da Nang, leaving behind a new wife and two young daughters, then aged 2 and 1, respectively, who would never see him alive again.

He'd grown up a devout family man, but Rodney Davis was also a true Marine, one who wasn't about to sit idly by in relative comfort while others did the fighting. If there were a conflict anywhere in the world involving his country, Davis and many other Marines like him believed it to be their solemn duty to be involved in the fray. He'd lived his entire life and never once shied away from a fight - he wasn't about to start now that he was in uniform.

Per his official orders, Davis first headed to Okinawa, Japan before making his way to Vietnam and reporting to 2nd Platoon, Bravo Company, the First Battalion, Fifth Marine Regiment (designated 1/5, which is pronounced "One Five"), First Marine Division upon arriving in country. All Marines were required to briefly stop in Okinawa to store their so-called "Sea-bags" that contained all the personal possessions they had brought with them. The Sea-bags were massed on the Japanese island and would usually catch up to the Marines a few months later. In the meantime, they were instead issued a small duffel bag containing several pairs of new socks and underwear before being quickly sent on their way to Vietnam. It was there that the Marines would receive their weapons and all the combat uniforms and other gear they would need.

Marines will tell you that nobody handles logistics better than the U.S. Marine Corps.

Nevertheless, Davis wasn't sure what to expect when the commercial 727 airliner carrying him and about 100 other Marines touched down in Da Nang.

He wound up spending a little more than a day there waiting for his paperwork to catch up with him before word finally came down that he and several other replacements were to hop a ride aboard an outgoing helicopter and join his new unit in the field.

The brief respite of sorts had served as an eye-opening experience to Davis about the violent new world now awaiting him. The long, traumatized faces of the many wounded making their way around the base spoke volumes. It was the taut look in their drawn-out eyes that had immediately grabbed Davis' attention. Often called a window to the soul, the forlorn look of the eyes of these wounded warriors spoke of a horrific nightmare from which they couldn't awake, instantly aging most of these young men well beyond their years.

But better that, Davis thought, than be going home in any one of the many silver, flag-covered coffins he saw being loaded aboard aircraft for transport home.

As he settled into his seat and awaited the start of the ride that would unite him with his new outfit, Davis suddenly felt a twinge of regret. His decision to leave Judy and the girls behind had seemed so easy at the time he had made it, but he was starting to have some initial doubts after arriving in Da Nang and seeing the ugly aftermath of war up close for the first time.

Davis had never until then really considered the possibility that he might actually die in Vietnam and never see his family again.

Yes, he'd spoken with his older brother about looking after his family in the event of such a possibility, but he never really believed for one second that such a thing might actually happen. It was only now that the very real possibility began to sink in with Davis.

"Did I make the right decision?" he asked himself. "Was it selfish of me to want to come to Vietnam?"

But any lingering doubts he may have had quickly dissolved because Davis remained supremely confident that nobody was better trained than he for the assignment ahead of him. He was sure that he was meant to be in Vietnam.

It had always been his destiny.

"There is nobody better trained for this than I am," he consistently thought to himself. "This is where I was supposed to be."

Davis kept reminding himself of that as the UH-1E helicopter began its ascent from the dusty tarmac, quickly lifting off into the deep blue sky to marshal him and the several other replacements aboard to their new home in the Que Son Valley.

****

Davis didn't have long to get acclimated to his new environment, and had only been in Vietnam for three weeks when the bloody Operation Swift began in the Que Son Valley in the early morning hours of Sept. 4, 1967. By the time it had finally concluded on Sept. 15, 114 Marines had been killed in the bitter fighting, with still hundreds more wounded, many of those seriously. Conversely, the operation resulted in the deaths of nearly 600 North Vietnamese Army (NVA) soldiers, according to U.S. military figures.

Roughly nine miles long and four miles wide, the Que Son Valley is orientated in a general northeast to southwest direction, split in half by the Song Ly Ly River from the northeast to southwest. The river provided a corridor that was the best avenue of approach into the mountains located to the west and southwest of the Marine combat base on Hill 51. The scenic mountains northwest of the combat base provided the enemy a natural easy escape route back into Laos.

The decision to locate the 1/5 at Hill 51 in May 1967 followed the earlier conclusion of Operation Union I. The Americans had made significant gains into controlling the valley in the fight and felt it important to maintain their presence so as to deny the enemy an opportunity to re-establish its presence. By the summer of 1967, the NVA and Viet Cong had been hurt badly by the two Union operations and had largely retreated back into sanctuaries in Laos and Cambodia in an effort to replenish their depleted numbers and get themselves combat ready again.

It's for that reason things had been relatively quiet in the Que Son Valley in three months following the conclusion of Operation Union II in early June 1967.

But before they could move into their new home, the now battle-tested and proven Marines were forced to eliminate a number of VC fighters still left in the area while chasing others away. But the area was still clearly bristling with enemy activity, so the Americans wasted no time in building the necessary gun emplacements, bunkers and other defensive works. It was imperative that they were quickly prepared for any eventuality.

The post's numerical name had little to do with any kind of strategic importance, but was instead a more sentimental choice by Peter L. Hilgartner, the lieutenant colonel commanding the 1/5 at the time. He had proudly worn No. 51 while playing high school football and was a member of the Naval Academy's Class of 1951. Now in command of the First Battalion, Fifth Marines, Hilgartner opted to designate the name of his new combat base as Hill 51, and the name stuck.

Located a little more than a half mile southwest of Que Son Village, the primitive post allowed the Marines to easily stay on top of everything going on in the valley. Its isolated location, however, meant that helicopter re-supply was the Marines' precious lifeline that was to be protected at all costs.

Populous and rich in rice, the Que Son Valley had long been recognized by the communists as strategically important to controlling the country's five northern provinces. By early 1967, at least two regiments from the NVA's 2nd Division had infiltrated the area, as the region's abundant food supply and seemingly endless source of conscripts had made retaining control of the

Que Son Valley one of their key objectives. The U.S. Military Assistance Command, Vietnam (MACV) had also recognized its importance and deployed the Fifth Marine Regiment to the valley as of May 1967 to support the outnumbered South Vietnamese Army (ARVN).

According to Hilgartner, the Marines' primary objectives in the area were to deny the VC and NVA access to the Que Son Basin and its vast food resources, provide the security needed for establishing civil action programs and force the Second NVA Division into open battle where U.S. technological and air superiority could win the day.

Marines from the 1st Battalion, 5th Marine Regiment on patrol in Vietnam's Que Son Valley in early September 1967. (photo courtesy of the Department of Defense)

Search-and-clear operations soon began in an effort to weed out the enemy and shield the local population from intimidation during upcoming elections. Davis was forced to learn quickly after arriving as daily patrols into the steamy jungles were followed by platoon- and squad-sized ambushes at night. The Marines rarely encountered their enemy in the immediate vicinity of their new fortified base, as the NVA preferred to keep the encounters small until they could replenish their numbers in the area.

But the climate remained tense as the Americans knew their every move was being watched.

"We never knew what we were going to run into when we went out," recalled Ed Burrow, a retired major who served as both the commander of 1st Platoon and Bravo Company's Executive Officer before his transfer to Headquarters Battalion in late August 1967.

The constant patrols and ambushes were a necessity to prevent a disaster by allowing the enemy to gather en masse right on top of them, but they left the Americans perilously thin back at the base, Burrow said. To mask their low numbers back at the base during patrols to the enemy eyes keeping an eye on them, the

Marines often employed dummies made of sandbags at positions along the perimeter. There were very few Americans left to defend the base and the 105mm and 81mm artillery batteries firing in support of the battalion from there should the communists have ever attacked.

With so much to do, the Marines consistently battled fatigue every bit as much as the stifling heat as they desperately sought to find the large NVA force hiding somewhere nearby amidst the overabundance of the valley's primary vegetation features of bamboo and scrub.

An eventual collision of the two opposing forces was just inevitable.

Operation Swift began just before sunrise on Sept. 4 when forces of the 1st NVA Regiment and elements of the 3rd and 21st Regiments suddenly attacked a considerably smaller Delta Company force on two sides just outside the village of Dong Son. Located about six kilometers southeast of the Marine combat base on Hill 51, Dong Son was little more than a cluster of hooches that sat on a low tree-lined rise close by and south of the Song Ly Ly River. Dong Son was adjacent to a huge rice paddy complex that included several square kilometers of active rice paddies and dikes on the north side of the village.

The landscape to the south consisted of low foothills, but the predominant terrain features in the area were similar to that of Dong Son and of nearby Chau Lam.

The 1/5 had been engaged in a company-sized search-and-destroy operation just a few kilometers east of the firebase when Delta Company had inadvertently stumbled into the superior-sized enemy force of about 2,500 men at about 4:30 a.m. in the pre-dawn dark of the morning of Sept. 4.

According to numerous Marine accounts, the deadly encounter began when one of the Delta Marines had stepped out of his position to go relieve himself in the early-morning darkness and inadvertently ran into an NVA soldier intent on doing likewise. It was the two startled men's subsequent shooting at one another that confirmed the nearby presence of the two, large opposing forces and precipitated the start of what would soon become one of the largest and deadliest operations of the entire Vietnam War.

Despite the battle's almost comical origins, the extensive network of trenches and well-dug and well-concealed fighting positions made it abundantly clear that the NVA forces had been in the area for a while.

It wasn't long before Delta, with its fewer than 200 men, was in danger of being overrun and in dire need of immediate help. Bravo Company, 1/5's lead company, soon received hasty orders to quickly mount up from their Hill 51 combat base in relief, but with the caveat to go light with extra ammunition. Bravo was the only immediate option for Marine firebase commanders, as all of Alpha Company was locked down in quarantine after breaking strict regulations and adopting a local dog as a pet that turned out to be rabid. Charlie Company remained well below strength following heavy casualties suffered during recent combat operations and was unavailable.

Retired and living in Northern Virginia until his death in late January 2015, Hilgartner remained irate for the remainder of his days about having gone into one of the fiercest battles of the entire Vietnam War without the services of one of his numerically stronger companies in Alpha Company because of something so silly and easily preventable. It was a known fact that dogs in Vietnam often came down with rabies and that the ailment wasn't always easily detected in its early stages. It was for that reason that Hilgartner had been very adamant from the outset in insisting that none of his Marines take any dogs in or adopt them as mascots. It was an egregious breakdown in discipline that ultimately cost American lives.

Hilgartner took small solace of sorts at the time in knowing that the intrusive rabies vaccinations into each man's stomach would hurt like hell. To further make his point, Hilgartner ordered the company commander to receive the dreaded shots along with his Marines to ensure the incident would never happen again.

But even that small consolation proved of little use to him when the early morning call came in saying that Delta Company was suddenly in a dire situation and in desperate need of immediate help. With Charlie Company still out of commission, the Bravo Marines were the only rifle company that Hilgartner had at his ready to send to Delta Company's aid. Two other 1/5 companies were on operational loan to another regiment at the time and unavailable, Hilgartner said.

The veteran battalion commander knew for certain that his Marines would be vastly outnumbered by the large enemy force known to have been lurking in the area, but he saw no other immediate alternative to preventing Delta Company's imminent slaughter.

"Bravo Company, saddle up!" quickly became the call throughout the combat base, reverberating down the line like falling dominoes as the Marines quickly spread the word by repeating the urgent call to action. Some of the young, weary Marines had just straggled into the mess hall following the earlier conclusion of night time combat patrols or all-night duty at the listening posts leading to the combat base and were only now beginning to sit down to eat breakfast. Others had already climbed into their bunks in the hopes of getting some much-needed sleep when word reached them and they immediately began rushing back to their respective platoon areas and gearing up.

Lance Corporal Gary Petrous said he immediately noticed a heightened sense of urgency he'd never witnessed before, not even on the prior occasions when he and his fellow Marines had served as a quick reaction force that had them always ready at a moment's notice. The Marines were normally afforded the luxury of being very meticulous in assembling their combat gear the night before going out on patrol.

Not this time.

Word quickly filtered through the ranks that Delta 1/5 had unknowingly set in the night before on the same hill that the NVA occupied and, when the sun came out, the NVA had come out of their holes to be right among them. The Bravo Marines were told that Delta was still involved in a desperate fight and that they were to go immediately to relieve them.

Davis, who had tasted combat for the first time two weeks earlier when Bravo Company had exchanged fire with a small group of Viet Cong it had encountered during an August 20th patrol, wasted no time jumping into action.

"Let's go, Marines!" he screamed to his men as they hastily scrambled to gather their gear. "Time to go right now! Delta needs our help!"

The Marines from Bravo Company left camp in a hurry just before 7 a.m., oblivious to just what kind of mayhem awaited them. They were under strict orders to go with light packs, meaning they were to carry no sleeping gear, but were to bring an extra pair of socks, a towel and as much ammunition and C-rations as they could carry. The Marines always made sure to carry full canteens with them, as a lack of available water while out in the field was always a problem. They took nothing else with them because they had to move quickly.

It would be shortly thereafter that the young Americans of both Bravo and Delta Companies would find themselves engaged with main enemy force in a fierce battle that would violently rage for more than 12 hours.

By the time the Bravo Company Marines left camp, the crisp, early morning light had already given way to the start of another bright, sunny day as the average high temperature during Operation Swift was 90 degrees with an average low of 75. Just like the previous several days before, Sept. 4 promised to again be hot, sticky and ripe with humidity with the prospect of the occasional late afternoon rain shower.

Shortly after their departure from the combat base to rush to the aid of their beleaguered comrades of Delta Company, the Bravo Company Marines noticed the two armed Huey gunships (UH-1E helicopters) equipped with deadly 40mm rocket pods attached flying overhead in the same direction in which they were also headed.

Some of the fresh-faced, newly-arrived Marines in the impromptu march took immediate solace in knowing they would have such heavy-duty ordnance so readily at their disposal. Other, more seasoned veterans took a more cynical view, asking quietly among themselves why such firepower was going to be needed in the first place. That's when they knew for sure that a nasty fight awaited them.

Davis and 2nd Platoon had assumed the point in the rush to aid their comrades, quickly following a stream east from their base to the site of the fighting. The company commander, Capt. Tom Reese, was all over the radio demanding they pick up the pace, prompting some complaints from within the ranks about the rapid speed of the march.

Some of the Bravo Company Marines worried that, in their haste to rush to the scene, they might inadvertently stumble into an NVA ambush before they even knew it and suddenly find themselves in equally-as-dire circumstances as well.

But it was a chance they had to take because time was of the essence. Delta Company's very survival depended on the prompt arrival of the Bravo Company Marines. Lives hung in the precarious balance with every passing second.

The weather was uncharacteristically cooperative during what was typically the start of Vietnam's rainy monsoon season, allowing the Marines to make quicker time. The wet conditions usual for that time of year typically limited offensive military operations as the flooded streams and rivers slowed ground movement, while dense fog and muddled conditions also played havoc with air cover.

Not so during Operation Swift, however, as the weather was consistently warm and humid, with occasional late afternoon showers and unrestricted visibility for the most part.

Soon after getting underway, the 2nd Platoon Marines came across the area where "Puff the Magic Dragon" had just made its lethal presence known to the enemy just a little while earlier in support of Delta Company. So nicknamed because of its lethal 7.62 millimeter mini-guns that could blast up to 3,000 rounds per minute and cover every square foot of a football field with one explosive round in a minute, the Douglas AC-47 gunship left a trail of death wherever it had been. Its every fifth round was a tracer bullet that was often referred to at night as "the red line of death" because it was built with a small, pyrotechnic charge in the base that lit up and became visible to naked eye, allowing the shooter to follow the projectile trajectory and easily make aiming corrections.

The red tracers were said to resemble fire coming from a dragon when fired at night, prompting the plane's infamous nickname from the Peter, Paul and Mary song from 1963.

There were large, visible holes in everything the Marines came upon. Trees, bushes, the ground and anything else that happened to be there when Puff began unleashing its fiery breath had all been cut down where it stood. There were visible blood trails, but the Americans found no enemy bodies, as the NVA had always been very careful to quickly remove their own dead or anything else as much as possible so as to not give evidence to the extent of the damage they had suffered.

But if there were any doubts as to their enemy's steely resolve, they dissipated soon afterwards when the Marines came across the burned out shell of an American Huey helicopter that had been shot down just a little while earlier.

The Americans nonetheless continued their march towards their beleaguered comrades in Delta Company.

Accurately realizing that this was going to become the major battle of his command, Hilgartner reached out to his regimental commander, Col. Stanley Davis, for additional help for his beleaguered Marines in their fight against what he knew to be a vastly numerically superior enemy force. Davis responded by giving Hilgartner operational control of Kilo and Mike companies from the Third Battalion, Fifth Marines.

Hilgartner was now ready to fully commit himself to the fight.

After crossing the local stream five or six times while en route, the Bravo Company Marines arrived in the vicinity of Delta Company at roughly 8:20 a.m. Their intent was to enter Delta's perimeter from the same side of the stream (north), only they had inadvertently entered on the wrong side and, instead, had wandered into the NVA's perimeter before anybody on either side had realized it.

The Marines were still unaware the NVA had pulled around to the east of Delta's lines by that point.

It worked out fortuitously as the Americans completely surprised the enemy forces still remaining in the area they'd stumbled upon. Davis was one of the roughly 13 men from 1st squad who came across a group of startled Viet Cong (VC) congregating together, each dressed in what was a very common black peasant shirt and pants outfit that more resembled pajamas.

"They were completely surprised," Posey said. "We were only slightly less surprised."

A brief, but spirited firefight immediately ensued, with Davis killing at least one of the communists - a girl of about 20 years of age – with a quick burst to the chest from his M16 rifle. He was still crouched over, combing over her body for maps and other potentially valuable intelligence when Posey and 3rd squad finally came upon the scene a minute or two later.

The Marines soon cleared the nearby 10 or so foxholes of the enemy forces that had been firing indiscriminately upon Delta Company. The area had only been secured for some five to 10 minutes when a hidden enemy soldier suddenly broke out from behind a brick building just behind the Marines and made a run for safety.

He didn't make it far as the 12 to 14 Marines present all quickly took aim and collectively brought him down with pinpoint rifle fire.

Bravo Company quickly resumed making its way to Delta's position in the hopes of accomplishing its stated mission and finally at last relieving the battered unit. An eerie quiet soon had settled over the entire area like a wet blanket by that time, leaving the scared Bravo Company Marines to begin thinking that maybe the surging NVA force had actually succeeded and overrun Delta Company during the fighting to make all their worst fears a reality.

But the two Marine companies soon made radio contact at just before 8:30 a.m., with Delta warning the incoming Marines to remain on the look-out for the large, well-equipped enemy force still lurking out there somewhere nearby. Now on highest alert, the Bravo Company Marines were slow and deliberate with their every step, with each of the young Americans fighting their every natural instincts to rush and duck for cover even as they could almost feel the presence of hidden enemy eyes gazing upon them.

"I was so scared the hair was standing up on my arms," Petrous recalled.

The Bravo Company Marines continued to surge forward and soon reached their comrades-in-arms before moving some 200 to 250 yards beyond Delta Company's perimeter to further check the area for additional enemy troops. They soon came to a tree line with an open field of about 100 yards when they immediately began taking fire.

The Americans quickly returned fire, aiming at the only things they see could through the thick jungle foliage in the exposed glints of metal, the moving trees and the ominous flashes of rifle fire aimed in their direction.

Two Marines had been hit before orders came over the radio to pull back, return to Delta's perimeter and leave the tree line to an incoming napalm strike.

Bravo Company had expected some stiff resistance in its relief efforts, but the Marines had no idea they'd soon be staring down an NVA force - one with a rare willingness to fight it out in a conventional manner with the more technologically sophisticated Americans.

The bulk of the most recent prior engagements against the NVA had entailed run-ins with small groups of enemy forces, leading some of the fresh-faced Americans new to the Que Son Valley to think that's how combat there would remain.

They couldn't have been more wrong about anything.

Additional large elements of the NVA and Viet Cong soon slipped back into the area joined the fray following a brief break in the fighting. Enemy units identified during Operation Swift included the 1st NVA Regiment, which consisted of the 40th, the 60th and the 90th Battalions. Each came with an estimated strength of 600 men per battalion, according to the 1/5 Combat After Action Report, and received additional men and supplies came from the 3rd and 21st NVA Regiments, as well as local Viet Cong forces. Total enemy strength was estimated to be 2,500 men.

It was around noon that Bravo Company again began receiving heavy automatic and semi-automatic fire from camouflaged enemy troops who were well dug in one of the three hamlets that comprised the village of Vin Huy.

After initially hearing the large volumes of gunfire in the near distance, Capt. Reese had expressed his displeasure to his company radio operator, Lance Corporal Rob MacNichol, about what he believed at the time to be 2nd Platoon's indiscriminate shooting and waste of ammunition.

They had all incorrectly assumed they'd already seen the last remnants of hostile fire from this particular combat action, and had by no means expected this latest foray to blow up into a full-blown battle. So Reese had just naturally assumed his Marines were only doing what they typically liked to do in that situation.

Namely, lightening the load they had to hump back to camp by blowing off ammunition.

So upon hearing additional volleys of gunfire moments later, an irate Reese quickly instructed MacNichol to contact 2nd Platoon with specific orders to quit firing at once.

It took 2nd Platoon's radio operator, Lance Corporal Gregory Crandall, to quickly bring his CO up to speed.

"That's not us," Crandall reported back. "That's them, and they're in line and making an assault."

Reese screamed back, "Tell them to return fire!"

Not that there was any need for such obvious instructions.

The well-prepared North Vietnamese were now everywhere the out-manned and out-gunned Marines could see. They came in platoon formation, filling the air everywhere with the hot steel from their Soviet-made mortars, machine guns and the AK-47 rifles they were bringing to bear from their hips.

Death was suddenly coming for the Marines in waves of three-man fire teams.

Soon facing the prospect of being completely overrun and annihilated, Reese coolly responded by calling in for some timely artillery-delivered teargas strikes on the fast-approaching enemy forces. Fortunately for the Americans, the NVA typically lacked gas masks at the time, so they usually backed up roughly a thousand meters or so at the sight of teargas as to elude its uncomfortable effects before regrouping and resuming its attack minutes later.

Reese's quick thinking under duress likely saved the lives of countless Marines, as the deployment of the tear gas allowed enough time for approaching reinforcements from the 3/5 Marines to arrive and for better coordination of the supporting artillery, helicopter gunship and jet fighter-bomber strikes that would save the day when the North Vietnamese assault resumed.

Reese was considered to be an excellent officer by those who served with him, and his mastery of the tactical use of combined arms has been credited with saving the lives of scores of Marines during the exceptionally violent first three days of Operation Swift. He knew just what arms to bring to bear against the on-rushing enemy forces and - equally as importantly - exactly when to do so.

Yet even that much-needed assistance proved deadly as the close-quartered nature of the day's ferocious hand-to-hand fight led to a number of inevitable friendly-fire casualties among the American ranks from the helicopter gunships and jets flying overhead with the intent of helping the Marines stay alive against a numerically superior force.

Following a devastating American airstrike on the enemy position, Davis and the rest of Bravo Company assaulted the position. The weakened NVA force retreated, with the Bravo Marines continuing to shoot at them while following in hot pursuit. Five Bravo Marines were killed and eight others wounded during the assault, according to the Combat After Action Report. Nine NVA soldiers were confirmed dead, while 35 others were labeled as probable KIAs. Two suspected Viet Cong were apprehended and turned over to intelligence.

It was suddenly a knock-down, no-holds-barred fight down to bayonets and rifle butts, and everything was fair game.

Bravo Company was hardly alone in its struggles just to stay alive that afternoon. Mike Lovejoy was a 21-year-old private first class serving as a radio operator for 2nd Platoon, Mike Company Third Battalion, Fifth Marine Regiment and had a front row seat to the copious amounts of airstrikes near his company position located roughly a thousand meters northwest of the Bravo Marines. The NVA had successfully cut off each of the four Marine companies on the field by the end of the day so as to prevent them from consolidating and formulating a stronger defense.

Persistent airstrikes with everything ranging from 250- to 1,000-pound bombs and napalm had been effective in preventing the NVA from overrunning the Mike Company Marines, but the enemy's effective ambush and superior numbers assured that all ground operations were in defensive nature alone.

But Lovejoy recalls one enemy anti-aircraft battery that had been ignored until near dark despite having proven particularly effective in denying the American jets the chance to drop ordnance where it would be most effective. It had now become imperative that the battery be taken out so that much-needed medevac and resupply helicopters could land.

Try as they might, the attacking American fighter/bombers had been forced to peel off on several tries in the face of the withering enemy fire aimed in their direction well before getting close enough to take the lethal enemy guns out. But some creative fighter jocks devised a wily plan of their own, much to the NVA's dismay.

It was near dark when a Navy F-4 Phantom began its run on the anti-aircraft site, only to be rudely greeted with murderous AA fire highlighted by green tracer rounds. As the F-4 drew close, the pilot turned on his bright landing lights and began turning away. As had been anticipated, the enemy AA fire followed the diverting plane, unaware that there was a second F-4 tucked up on the tail of the first.

Taking advantage of the AA gunners' focus on his partner, the second F-4 pilot followed the tracer fire back to its source and perfectly delivered a 500-pound bomb that forever silenced the enemy battery and the enemy soldiers manning it to the many cheers from the Marines on the ground.

Lovejoy said that he and other Marines immediately began jumping out of their bomb craters "yelling and cheering like we won a football game."

Similar scenes of life and death played out throughout the Que Son Valley that day as the outnumbered Marines desperately fought for their very lives.

After sustaining heavy losses, the NVA had hastily retreated north across the Song Ly Ly to regroup late in the afternoon, allowing the Marines time to tend to their own dead and wounded. It also provided the time necessary for all of the 3/5 Marines from M and K companies to arrive in the vicinity and fully deploy.

While Bravo Company had been fighting on the east side of the village that morning, Marine helicopters had arrived on the scene to carry out Delta Company's dead and wounded. The NVA had deceitfully used decoy smoke signals to lure them in even closer before opening fire with small arms fire and bringing down two aircraft to add to the rising casualty total.

Lovejoy was among the just 10 Marines left standing of the 45 to start the day in 2nd Platoon, Mike Company by the end of the day. He and the remaining Marines were placed in 1st and 3rd Platoons for the remainder of Operation Swift.

Compounding Mike Company's problems were repeated glitches with the new M16E1 rifles the Marines had only begun using a few months earlier, Lovejoy said. A design flaw led many of them to jam and leave Marines too often unable to adequately defend themselves against the hard-charging NVA attack. Lovejoy estimated that 50 percent of his company's casualties could be directly attributed to the malfunctioning rifles that frequently jammed and wouldn't fire following the firing of one round. Desperate to stave off the large enemy force advancing on their position, the young Americans were forced to switch rifles after the firing of each round, passing the one that had just been used back to a Marine standing behind them whose job it was to quickly clean them out so that they may be used again.

The lack of firing efficiency denied the Americans the opportunity to go fully automatic against the mass of NVA soldiers headed their way.

It wasn't until late 1967 that all Marines had been issued the improved M16A1 rifle.

Delta Company had also been decimated by the fierce combat, reduced in strength by 25 percent following the conclusion of the first day of Operation Swift, Hilgartner said. Fourteen Delta Marines were killed that day, including company commander Capt. Robert F. Morgan, while 15 others had been wounded in action.

Prior to his own arrival in Vietnam, Morgan had been Sgt. Rodney M. Davis' first commanding officer in London.

By the end of Sept. 4th, 54 Marines overall had been killed with another 104 wounded, according to the Combat After Action Report, making it the deadliest single day during the 1/5's tenure of the entire Vietnam War.

Among the many dead were Navy lieutenant Vincent Capodanno, the beloved chaplain who had disregarded his own wounds to tend to the dying and wounded when an NVA machine gun struck him down. More affectionately known as "The Grunt Padre" because of his desire to always be along the front lines living and eating with his Marines, Capodanno had overheard reports that Mike Company's 2nd Platoon was in danger of being overrun and had sought permission to join the Marines in their time of need. He ignored orders to stay in the rear and instead hitched a helicopter ride to the front lines where he joined 2nd Platoon. He was attempting to cover a downed corpsman when he was killed.

Capodanno, who had previously served with the 1/5 until being assigned to the 3/5 in July, was later posthumously awarded the Medal of Honor for his actions. News of his death, however, came as a blow to the entire battalion. Capodanno is among the nine chaplains in U.S. military annals to have been awarded the Medal of Honor.

In another very unusual twist, Capodanno was among the two Medal of Honors to originate that day from 2nd Platoon, Mike Company. Sgt. Lawrence D. Peters was the other Marine to later be posthumously awarded the nation's highest military honor for valor following his actions that afternoon. Peters had repeatedly stood in the open despite the withering NVA fire aimed in his direction to point out enemy positions to his men and direct their fire. He continued to do so even after suffering additional wounds until eventually losing consciousness and succumbing to his injuries.

Heroes abounded everywhere, making uncommon valor a common virtue in the day's horrific conditions.

The Marines from Delta Company would soon be limping back to base to recover, so it was left up to Bravo Company to fill in its perimeter for that evening. During the transition, a fleet of Marine resupply helicopters were feverishly hauling in needed additional food and ammunition. No shots were fired at any point during the process, leading many of the Bravo Marines to erroneously assume that the worst was over, that the NVA had withdrawn from the area following the day's heavy fighting and that only cleanup operations remained ahead.

There isn't a long twilight in Vietnam, so it got dark quickly by the time the sun finally went down. The bloodied Americans looked to regroup as night descended upon them.

****

The mission of the Bravo Company Marines had now changed after starting the day with the primary intent of rescuing their endangered comrades from Delta Company. Rather than just return to base, the Marines were ordered to head south to chase and engage the large enemy force still known to be lurking in the area.

All the Marines tried to relax as much as possible following the day's lengthy pitched battle while knowing there was likely more bitter fighting to come.

But there was still work to be done in the meantime.

As 2nd platoon's right guide, Davis was the unit's third-highest ranking member, behind only Brackeen, the platoon commander, and platoon sergeant Ron Posey. As such, Davis served as the platoon's administrative arm whose chief responsibilities were to dole out supplies to his troops as required. That entailed maintaining consistent contact with both Brackeen and Posey at all times, as well all squad leaders for any supplies they might have suddenly needed.

Ammunition, food, boots, fresh socks, cigarettes or whatever else.

"I think it was an impossible task without a radioman with him at all times," Posey said, "but Rodney did it. I can't imagine that he had much free time."

It hadn't been easy earning the grudging respect of the many grizzled Marines who had already been in the valley for a few months and had seen heavy action in the previous campaigns of Operations Union, Union II, Adair, Calhoun and Cochise. Davis, however, had quickly begun establishing his own bona fides soon after his arrival a few weeks earlier, recalled Ben Drollinger, a 2nd Lieutenant with Bravo Company's 1st Platoon.

Drollinger, who had just arrived in Vietnam in June, had met Davis for the first time only a few days before. The young lieutenant had been medevaced out to a hospital on Aug. 10 after being shot and didn't return to the dangerous front lines in the Que Son Valley until Aug. 29.

Davis was one of the three newly-arrived sergeants Drollinger had made a point of quickly getting to know. Bravo Company had been devastated by casualties during previous combat operations, leaving several corporals as the ranking non-commissioned officers (NCOs) in the absence of all the other veteran sergeants who had either been killed or wounded.

Often called the backbone of any platoon, an E-5 (Sergeant) is the glue that holds the unit together on a daily basis while also educating the young troops and holding everybody accountable. Impressionable young soldiers often follow his lead.

Davis had quickly established himself as fit for such an awesome responsibility, and showed it by example on a daily basis in the high professional manner in which he carried himself and challenged his men to do likewise. The platoon quickly caught on that he was the intense, no-nonsense type who accepted no excuses. Quiet by nature, Davis was always in firm control of things asked of him and made certain his gear and everything about his person was always in perfect order. He wouldn't tolerate any of his charges failing to complete their daily assigned duties, and he made sure they consistently cleaned their weapons properly and always looked and behaved like Marines.

Good enough wouldn't do. Everything had to be just right because Davis knew all their lives could soon depend on it.

"He was squared-away in a short period of time," Drollinger said. "He was very well-respected. He looked out for his people."

His Marines thought Davis to be tough, but always fair and very clear about the expectations he had of them.

"Everybody liked him," Lance Corporal Lonnie R. Hinshaw said.

His litany of duties kept Davis constantly busy, so much so that he only had time to write home once after arriving in country. In a brief letter dated Aug. 19, 1967, Davis sounded optimistic about his new posting.

"Dearest Judy,

Just a few lines to let you know that I am doing OK and think I'm going to like it here, only if I get used to being filthy with dirt. It's impossible to get clean.

I hope this letter finds you and the children doing fine. Kiss them for me. I love you and them and miss you all.

How do you like this new paper I'm writing on? See, I told you it wasn't going to be all that bad, and we have just moved up on this Hill

51 [for] support. [Hill 51] seems to have a little history behind it. I hope they don't have any in the future.

Tell Mom and Daddy I said hello and the rest of the people.

I guess I will close here. Be sweet and remember I love you with all my heart and always will.

With all my love.

Rod"

That would be the last thing his family would ever hear from him.

A 19-year-old lance corporal serving as an assistant machine gunner in 2nd Platoon at the time, Petrous would see an inordinate amount of time at the tip of the spear of heavy combat action during his 13-month tour of duty in Vietnam as a rare survivor of both Operations Union I and II, Operation Swift and what he sarcastically calls "a farewell tour through Hue City" during the Tet Offensive of early 1968. The easy-going Michigan native insists that Operation Swift accounted for the worst three days of his entire tour.

Petrous didn't know Davis personally, but still vividly remembers the worn-out look on his face as he walked by his foxhole shortly following the conclusion of the major combat operations of Sept. 4.

"Tough day?" Petrous asked in the brief, but only conversation of any sort ever shared by the two men.

"Whew!" Davis responded, shrugging his shoulders as he allowed a warm smile across his face and moved on to his next assigned task.

Davis had already completed his main objective that Sept. 4 evening of making sure to replace the many grenades the platoon had used in battle earlier in the day when he and Brackeen would speak for the last time. The two men and Posey had found themselves beside one another in a shallow foxhole as they consolidated their defensive positions for the night.

Such an assemblage wasn't uncommon along the front lines, as platoon leaders easily spent more time together with their senior NCOs than they did with anybody else, other officers included. So much that Drollinger likes to say now that he knew his senior NCOs in Vietnam better than he did his own brother.

The NCOs typically had considerably more field and combat experience than the many novice lieutenants often leading the platoons, so it always behooved the young officers to listen to what they had to say.

In combat, that shared knowledge could often mean the difference between life and death.

"How are we looking?" Brackeen asked his two sergeants.

"We're good, sir," Posey responded. "Everybody's where they need to be."

Davis nodded in agreement, as an eerie silence settled in over the three weary men like a dense fog. There was always something else to be done, but neither Davis, Brackeen nor Posey had the heart for it at that late point in the day. The day had been unforgettably horrific, complete with vicious hand-to-hand combat that had resulted in the gruesome deaths of so many young Marines.

There was nothing anybody could say to assuage the raw emotions they were feeling at that moment, especially with the prospect of more close-quarters fighting looming ahead. All the young Americans could do was try to get a handle on all they'd already seen and endured the best they could in the short time they had.

They were Marines and still had a job to do.

Several minutes had passed by when Brackeen finally broke the ice.

"Sgt. Davis, I'm guessing you never had days like this in London," the lieutenant said. "How did you enjoy your time there anyway?"

Davis appeared somewhat stunned by the question, by its timing as much as its more personal nature. He and Brackeen had enjoyed a very good working relationship in the few weeks since he'd arrived in country, but their conversations had typically been brief and had never previously been of the personal nature.

Davis quickly gathered himself.

"It was great, sir," he answered. "It was a really great experience and it's where I met my wife Judy. She and our two baby girls are back in Macon now with my family. I can't wait to get back home to see them all again."

"Yeah, I know how you feel, sergeant," Brackeen said, nodding in agreement before turning to Posey and inquiring about his family. "I miss my family, too."

The tension broken, Davis soon began speaking in much greater detail of his previous tour of duty at the U.S. Embassy in London, his marriage there, the couple's two small daughters and his close-knit family back in Macon, especially his siblings. Posey also spoke of his own family and the wife awaiting his return.

The reality is that all three men likely understood that personal specifics were of little consequence to anybody at that moment in the Que Son Valley. The dialogue, however, was critical in helping each man to at least temporarily put aside the horrors of earlier in the day for more pleasant thoughts. It also served as another stark reminder for what they were fighting.

The conversation didn't last particularly long as the battle-weary Marines soon began eating their rations, drinking all the water they could and trying to sleep in turn as much as was possible. The Americans remained on high alert and couldn't afford to be distracted with conversation for lengthy periods of time. Their very lives depended on it.

Illumination flares from C-47s flying overhead kept the area lit up all night, but sporadic gunfire and outgoing Marine artillery sailing over their heads to hammer nearby enemy strongholds throughout the night served as additional chilling reminders as to not get too comfortable just yet. In fact, it was Brackeen who volunteered that it was probably not a good idea in the first place that the three highest-ranking men in the platoon were simultaneously sharing the same foxhole. All it would take, he explained, would be one well-placed enemy mortar round in their direction to suddenly render 2nd Platoon a rudderless ship ripe for disaster.

Nevertheless, it would be one of the few times the 2nd Platoon Marines and Davis would engage in such personal small talk during his short time in Vietnam. That they did so at all perhaps speaks volumes to what life is often like in a tense combat zone, say those who know best.

Lots of stomach-wrenching anxiety from the long, torturous periods of waiting, punctuated by the few moments of extremely intense and unforgettable violence.

The young Marines were keenly aware of the kind of violent storm still brewing ahead and desperately grasped at anything to help them pass the time. It was rare that anybody ever spoke specifically about the possibility of dying, but it was always understood that such a prospect was never far off. The inherent danger of their jobs meant it was probably best to keep some personal distance from most of the others.

Remaining focused was imperative for one's own survival.

That was especially true for Brackeen and Posey, both of whom faced the daunting prospect of giving orders they knew would eventually lead to the deaths of some of their men. As an officer, it was critically important for Brackeen to keep some professional and personal space so that he might easier make those hard decisions at decisive times.

A Texas native who had been in command of the platoon since May, Brackeen was what Marines call a "Mustang" because he had been on both sides after first enlisting in the Marine Corps at age 17 and later going to Officer Candidates School (OCS) to receive a commission.

After completing two tours of duty in Vietnam, he would leave the Marine Corps for good in 1969.

Despite the inherently potential hazards, the lieutenant had taken it upon himself to find out a little something about each of the men in his platoon. The decision to do so was his own personal choice, but it was also information he knew he would inevitably need when some of his men were killed and he had to write condolence letters home to their families. A notebook Brackeen kept on him at all times contained personal information on all of his men, such as the name of their wives, as well as each of their various hometown addresses, next of kin, blood type and service numbers.

That information would come in handy later when the wounded lieutenant wrote condolence letters to both Davis' wife and mother from a hospital room in Japan in the immediate days following Rodney's death.

That same professional distance is just what Posey also had in mind after being posted to 2nd Platoon just days earlier on Aug. 29. Davis had joined the platoon at roughly the same time, but Posey boasted a little more seniority. His six extra months of sergeant's stripes meant the job of platoon sergeant went to him rather than to Davis, who instead became the platoon's right guide.

At 28, Posey was easily the oldest man in the platoon, and he had quickly come to rely on that certain level of personal detachment.

"It's hard to send men to what might be their deaths," he said. "It's impossible to send friends, and the mission comes first."

Posey had only known Davis for just a brief time prior to his death, and the two men never had time to sit and really talk in depth during the short period they did serve alongside one another. But Posey vividly remembers Davis as a tall and friendly guy always ready with an easy smile.

He also recalled his calm and business-like approach to things.

It was an attribute that would soon serve Davis and the rest of the Bravo Company Marines well.

By the morning of Sept. 5, the NVA had broken off contact and pulled out, eerily leaving only their own dead where they fell in the field as the only proof they were ever there. Hilgartner had been unsuccessful in his pleas with his superiors to continue pursuing the NVA so that they might not get the chance to regroup. He felt that his Marines had the enemy on the ropes and saw what he believed to be a golden opportunity to completely destroy the large NVA force in the valley once and for all.

Hilgartner said his entreaties were rebuffed because higher-ups in command were demanding an NVA body count to give Washington, meaning the Marines had no choice but to cease their advance and count the number of enemy killed or captured, as well as tally the number of NVA and VC weapons that had been recovered. The war was being fought politically, as much as it was militarily.

"If it were up to me, I would have gone all the way to Hanoi," Hilgartner said.

The pause in the fighting allowed the bureaucrats desperate for more positive spin on the war's progress the precious time they required to feed a substantial enemy body count to the press and politicians back in Washington. But it proved equally as responsible for allowing the NVA the critical time it needed to bring up critical replacements and reorganize its forces for another offensive.

It's not a stretch to say that the untimely delay ultimately cost the lives of many Americans.

As a result, the fighting continued to be just sporadic throughout the day of September 5th for Bravo Company as Marine artillery continued to shell nearby enemy strongholds. Davis and Bravo took the time to regroup somewhat, while remaining ever vigilant.

Delta Company's nightmare was over, but Bravo's was only just beginning.

CHAPTER 9
DEATH IN THE TRENCHES

Their brief lull of sorts in major combat operations didn't last long, however, as Hilgartner issued an order on Sept. 6 directing the Marines to advance on Chau Lam. The small village was located eight kilometers east of Que Son and only about two kilometers east of the initial battlefield of two days earlier in Dong Son.

Davis and his fellow Bravo Company Marines embarked from their makeshift encampment, humping out at roughly 11 a.m. on Sept. 6 with specific instructions to pursue and engage the enemy. But there was little reason at that point to think they were on their way to doing just that, as the NVA had in the past consistently tried to avoid any prolonged direct engagement with a technologically superior American force that enjoyed major advantages in air and artillery support.

The Marines, however, desired nothing more than to lure them out into the open. Little could they imagine how quickly they would soon get their wish.

A clear sky helped the temperature quickly rise to a balmy 90 degrees by the time the Marines had begun their eastwardly march of about three kilometers in search of the large NVA force they knew to be lurking somewhere in the vicinity.

Understandably, accounts have varied in the 50 years that have passed about what exactly what happened next as memories fade.

Posey specifically recalled Bravo Company being slowed down for about two critical hours after receiving an order to exhume a mass grave the Marines discovered. Battalion command wanted to know just whose bodies they were, how many there were and how it was they died.

"I turned out to be a stupid order, and we would really need those hours we wasted on body count," Posey said.

Brackeen, however, remained adamant that his platoon had exhumed the bodies the day before - on Sept. 5 - and that his former platoon sergeant was simply mistaken. He recalled sniper fire that resulted in the wounding of a Marine that succeeded in slowing down his outfit. The Combat After Action Report chronicled such an event happening at 11:35 that morning.

All parties, however, were in agreement about what came next as Davis and his Bravo Company Marines carefully made their way into Chau Lam. The area had obviously just been bombed recently, as the many large, water-filled, bomb craters littering the entire vicinity so clearly testified. But other, more ominous signs screamed out to the Americans from the outset of their arrival, not the least of which was the fact that the small village was eerily quiet and completely devoid of all residents. A North Vietnamese flag was still flapping freely in the slight breeze, perched some 18-20 feet in the air atop a flagpole in an open area in the village center.

The abundance of tables in the eerily vacant village center led Posey to initially believe that it might have simply been the spot where the village children were taught school, but he quickly concluded the area had just recently been used as a staging area for NVA troops.

The deserted hammocks nearby and the recently prepared food still sitting out on tables only made all the Marines more acutely aware their enemy had only just abruptly left. Everybody knew for sure the NVA still had to be nearby and likely following their every move.

Bravo Company quickly came upon the village bunker where a small cadre of "scared shitless" civilians had fled for safety.

"There was a reason why they were so scared," Posey said.

The terrified family of six had taken refuge in the bunker, staying hidden and refusing to come out even after their presence had initially been discovered. An ARVN soldier on the scene screamed for all those inside to come out, but to no avail. When they still refused, the ARVN soldier tossed a grenade into the bunker to expedite the family's hasty exit out before shepherding them to safety.

None of the rescued family members ever mentioned a single word about the large NVA force lying in wait nearby for the Americans.

Hot, bothered and hungry after an eventful morning with temperatures having already climbed to roughly 100 degrees, the weary Marines of 2nd Platoon began to eat on the go after finally securing the village. They never stopped to eat at any time during Operation Swift, electing to eat on the move so as to never become a sitting target.

Contrary to public opinion, the Marines mostly liked the C-rations given to them, usually consisting of a variation of baked beans, lima beans, ham and some type of stew to go with a hearty dessert of fruit cocktail or a piece cake, Posey recalled.

They began leaving the village to resume their search for enemy forces by mid-afternoon, following a trail down a nearby hill through a cemetery and to the edge of a large rice paddy just outside the village, where the rest of the company awaited. The cemetery appeared to be a Buddhist one, with its round and completely symmetrical graves that weren't dug all that deep. They lacked tombstones, but were particularly distinctive by their accompanying mounds of dirt, most of which were neatly elevated roughly six to eight inches above the ground.

The scene outwardly appeared quite peaceful and serene, but the Marines knew better. Their orders were very clear – they were to push onwards and engage the enemy.

Yet the Americans had no way to guess their unseen enemy already had them within their sights, waiting only on them to unknowingly waltz into their previously-designated kill zone.

That critical moment came quickly as Bravo Company soon began crossing the paddy, with Davis, Posey, Brackeen, Leedom and the rest of 2nd Platoon following closely behind 1st Platoon.

Second Platoon had intended to cross the "island," turn right and cross another small paddy into a small village. The platoon had reached its designated turn point, while 1st Platoon was already square in the middle of the rice paddy just outside the small village, completely out in the open and unprotected when all hell broke loose.

Withering NVA small arms, rifle, mortar and heavy machine gun fire suddenly erupted from seemingly out of nowhere as the Marines had essentially walked into a deadly ambush set by a cunning enemy that had skillfully lured them into its snare.

Caught completely by surprise with nowhere to seek cover, a number of Marines were immediately killed or wounded. Also fatally cut down in the sudden murderous hail of bullets were the two Vietnamese prisoners that 2nd Platoon had been escorting.

Rounds were now zipping everywhere through the air in search of their targets, kicking up dirt as they missed and passed by harmlessly to further herald their deadly presence.

"An NVA regiment set a trap," Brackeen said, "and we walked into it. That's what happened. They knew we were coming."

As further proof, Brackeen cited the sniper attack earlier in the day that resulted in the wounding of a Marine. It was rather typical, he noted, of the NVA to employ such effective tactical measures to slow down American ground advances by making them wait for their wounded to be med-evaced out before moving on. The critical additional time allowed the NVA to better deploy their defenses or get away all together.

Whatever the circumstances leading to it, there was no doubting that an isolated Bravo Company had suddenly found itself in a very bad way. The unsuspecting Marines of 1st Platoon had been hit especially hard in the vulnerable open rice paddy, suffering nearly 100 percent casualties well before the day's end. Their lead four-man fire team and the machine gunner from their second fire team had been instantly slaughtered by a cluster of AK-47-toting North Vietnamese soldiers who were disciplined enough to wait until their prey was right on top of them before literally popping up out of the ground and opening up at close range.

Hidden from prying eyes by well-placed layers of bamboo and leaves, these so-called "spider traps" offered little chance of survival to those caught unaware. The lairs, which were carved several feet deep and wide enough to easily conceal the lurking enemy soldier inside, usually blended in perfectly with the rugged terrain of the surrounding rice paddies and were often difficult for Marines to spot from afar even when they weren't already under heavy fire.

The sudden chaos of combat just made it easier for the wily death traps to claim more unsuspecting victims.

It was always just understood the holes would be where the extremely dedicated North Vietnamese soldiers inside would also die because they had nowhere to run or hide after exposing themselves. But they didn't care as long as they first killed as many of the imperialist Americans as possible.

Their insidious plan worked perfectly on this day.

"They were the masters of the ambush," Drollinger said, "and we basically got smacked."

Agreed Petrous: "It was THE worst ambush. They had us 10 ways from Sunday."

Captain Reese, the company commander, was bleeding badly and out of commission after being shot in the lower abdomen soon after the bullets began flying. He was eventually med-evaced out the next morning, leaving Drollinger to assume control of Bravo Company after his commanding officer went down.

Sadly, Reese had been scheduled to rotate back to the U.S. in the upcoming days. His departure was so imminent that his replacement had already arrived, only to be told to stand down with the advent of the heavy fighting. Reese had wisely reasoned that a pitched battle between his U.S. Marines and a large force of crack NVA regulars was no time to break in a novice company commander. The troops in the field needed an experienced leader who could think and act quickly and decisively during the crucible of combat.

Reese's decision likely saved countless American lives.

In the meantime, the heavy volume of shooting sent all of the startled Marines darting for cover wherever they could find it.

"Everybody got down, either on their knees or on their belly," Posey said. "We looked outwards to see first where [the enemy fire] was coming from. The lieutenant got the message over the radio telling the platoon to move to another position so we could better return fire."

Bedlam isn't all that unusual in the initial moments of an unexpected attack, Drollinger explained.

"When the bad guys open fire, they usually rip through several magazines while our guys go flat and scramble for position," he said. "Within minutes, the troops normally settle down, the senior man controls radio traffic, the forward observer calls in artillery and helicopters and the enemy rate of fire slackens."

Drollinger proved himself an excellent leader, especially after having taken over in such dire conditions. His quick thinking and decisive tactical decisions following the loss of Reese prevented a disaster of epic proportions and saved countless Marine lives. Drollinger was later awarded the Silver Star for valor to go along with the four Purple Hearts he amassed during his tenure in Vietnam.

But this was unlike any other previous battle these Marines had ever experienced.

Despite heavy enemy fire, 2nd Platoon managed to navigate left to an open field and moved down to the edge of the paddy so it could cover an exposed 1st Platoon. It was a very poor tactical position as it angled away to the left, denying the Marines a view along the far right edge without exposing themselves to the barrage of NVA fire from their right.

Enemy soldiers sensing an opportunity began crossing the rice paddy en masse towards 2nd Platoon's right. The NVA had simultaneously begun laying heavy cover fire from the platoon's left front in the hopes of flanking the Americans.

Deadly American artillery strikes soon began raining down on the advancing horde, but the NVA continued to push forward. The communists knew it necessary to advance quickly to close the distance between themselves and their enemies to negate the effective American weapons barrage blistering them from above.

They inched ever closer to the Marines, as green NVA tracer fire and returning American red rounds lit up the sky.

"The position was not a good one," Brackeen said. "It was a bad position. They had cover in the form of branch and trees right up to our lines. It was a bad position, untenable."

Heavily outnumbered, 2nd Platoon nonetheless managed to repel several NVA assaults from across the rice paddy at its position, but it quickly became obvious the enemy's superior numbers made the Americans' position a precarious one. Sensing potential disaster, Brackeen ordered his Marines to pull back to the edge of the field where there was a tree line and a large bomb crater. They took immediate cover in a 30-foot long trench along the tree line, buffered by the 100 yards of open field in the form of the rice paddy in front of them and the roughly 200 yards of thick woods that stretched along their right front.

The muddy trench from which the Marines were now fighting for their lives was one of thousands built along tree lines throughout the country over the course of the constant warfare that had ravaged Vietnam throughout the previous 20 years. Another network of trenches in the woods provided the NVA the cover it needed to help close in on the heavily outnumbered Americans.

Such rudimentary methods of warfare may have initially appeared archaic in the nuclear age at the height of the ongoing Cold War between the U.S. and Soviet Union, but they had proven to be extremely effective. They were instrumental in helping in the defeat of the French years earlier, and the NVA and Viet Cong were hoping for a similar endgame against the Americans.

Heavy fighting had soon also engulfed the trail to the right by which 2nd Platoon had earlier traveled as 1st and 3rd platoons were likewise engaged against the numerically superior NVA force that was unrelenting in its waves of attack.

Brackeen was furiously working the radio in the hopes of getting the additional air support he and his men would need to survive.

The scene was one of absolute chaos, as there were so many men yelling amidst the dissonance of shooting and screaming. The bodies of the dead and wounded littered the ground, but there was no time to tend to such matters. None of the Marines' survival was certain.

Soldiers who have experienced the terror of combat will tell you that all you hear is a crack or pop in the air when a round is shot in your direction.

On this day, there were a bevy of such ominous noises.

"Everything happened so fast," Leedom recalled. "You were trying to kill somebody before they killed you."

Combat veterans will tell you that being in a firefight is by far THE most intense thing they've ever endured. The life-and-death gravity of the situation inherently means all of your senses are amped up like never before, with each man's heartbeat racing a million miles a minute and his mouth soon becoming parched dry from gut-wrenching fear and nervous anticipation.

Yet combat often appears to take place in slow motion, as each man's eyes become laser-focused in search of even the slightest of movements that might give away the enemy, their ears locked in on even the most seemingly innocuous of sounds.

Those who have withstood its intensity up close say that war is like nothing else they've ever experienced. It speaks volumes about its complexity that Posey says now that he hated all that he saw and endured in combat, while also adding that he wouldn't trade the intensity of the experience for anything.

Battles are characterized by deadly bullets filling up the air in search of their target, but those who have managed to elude them for an extended period of time come to know their unique calling card. By the time his tour was over, Petrous had become an expert of sorts of knowing which bullets flying over and around his body were perilously close and which weren't.

It was understood by everybody that death was never that far off in Vietnam.

"Whenever they were real close, they would make a snapping sound when they went by you," Petrous recalled. "If they were whizzing, they were usually high in the air. Sometimes, I would swear that I actually saw the ones that came really close to me. It was if they were going by in slow motion."

Combat veterans will tell you that they can still hear all the horrific screaming and yelling, the rapid firing of rifles and the chronic cracking of incoming rounds. Just the sound of a footstep on a nearby branch often served as the equivalent of touching a live 110-volt wire.

Posey can to this day still recall the rank smell of his own body and that of other Marines that was par for the course after being out in the field for several days without a shower, as much as he has never been able to shake the pungent smell of the chicken feces in which they were standing and that from the water buffaloes nearby. The precariousness of their life-and-death situation meant that Posey's amplified senses could clearly distinguish each smell and sound.

Nothing, however, is as unforgettable as the sweet, sickening aroma of blood. That horrific smell was everywhere on this day.

The bullets had just begun flying everywhere when a round suddenly cut through Posey's trousers, just missing his leg. But the close call immediately brought him to grips with the seriousness of the situation in which suddenly found himself, and the stark realization that there was a pretty good chance he wouldn't be making it out of the fight alive.

He hesitated for just a split second, wondering how his wife of roughly five years would make do in the event of his death and how his siblings would take the news. The whiz of bullets skimming just inches over his head, however, promptly snapped him out of it and ensured that his thoughts returned to the battle raging about him.

Posey moved on and continued to do what he needed to do in order to survive, having reached an inner peace of sorts with the death he believed to have been awaiting him.

In the meantime, he and the rest of the outnumbered Marines continued to desperately stave off the oncoming enemy forces. The 3/5 Marines from Kilo and Mike Companies were likewise simultaneously engaged in a fierce fight for their very lives at nearby enclaves, as the hand of death had descended upon the Que Son Valley.

If there were ever such thing as hell on earth, this would have been it.

It quickly became imperative that 2nd Platoon prevent the NVA from reaching the corner of the woods about 20 yards to the platoon's right front so as to deny the enemy the opportunity to flank the Marines and cut the company in two. With Brackeen pinned down in the bomb crater about 100 feet behind the trench, Davis had recognized just how critical things had become.

Incoming bullets were snapping over his head, hissing through the air all about him when he suddenly made a unilateral decision to brave the torrent of enemy fire and move up and down the line from man to man in the trench. Davis paid the immediate danger little mind, doing his best to encourage his fellow Marines in the hopes they'd buck up against the superior enemy numbers, hold their ground and temper the fast-charging NVA assault.

Panic had already begun to set in among some of the young, shell-shocked Marines and the real possibility of a disorganized retreat was imminent. Such a disastrous scenario most likely would have resulted in an even greater loss of more American lives, according to those on the ground, while perhaps even tipping the scale of the entire battle for control of the strategically important valley if something weren't done at that critical juncture.

Sensing the gravity of the situation, Davis took it upon himself to deploy his men into better tactical locations and re-direct 2nd Platoon's returning base fire. The ever-desperate Marines could see movement in the woods and shot at everything that moved.

Davis moved up and down the line to reassure his scared Marines in the face of the oncoming enemy onslaught.

"We've got good position now!" he repeated over and over. *"We've got guys where we need them and we're going to be OK!"*

He had suddenly taken control of a situation that was becoming more precarious by the minute. Just as he had so readily done on behalf of his siblings on so many occasions while growing up in Macon under the unforgiving boot of Jim Crow. Davis had always stood ready to look out after his own.

"His job wasn't to direct fire in combat," Posey said of Davis, "but, in the situation we were in, he just naturally did it. He had recognized a weak spot in our lines that was very important, and, if they had broken our lines there, the outcome would have been different for many that survived. There are many that owe Rodney a lot."

Leedom couldn't recollect just how it was that he came to be standing side-by-side with Davis in the muddy trench they shared. Fate, it seemed, had its own plans, as many unforeseen things often occur in the confusion that is the fog of war. It's commonplace for men involved in the same battle to recall the same experience differently as each individual frantically fights for his own survival in his own small corner of the conflict with little time for thought of any bigger picture.

Leedom was just such a case in point following his return to the field just a few days earlier after a stay in the hospital with a bout of malaria. A squad leader within 2nd Platoon, Leedom had never even been formally introduced to Davis prior to the start of Operation Swift. The two men had never even shared as much as a conversation prior to being indelibly linked by that fateful Sept. 6, 1967 afternoon.

"I knew who he was by sight," Leedom recalled. "He was a sergeant; I was a Lance Corporal. He was in charge."

In his haste to get out of the hospital following a bout with malaria and back out among his close friends, the young Marine affectionately nicknamed "Stickman" for his slight build hadn't been able to procure the full allotment of ammunition and supplies already given out to the rest of the platoon prior to the start of operations. Leedom was carrying just three magazines with 18 rounds apiece on him when the fighting started and quickly ran out of ammunition during the intense firefight. Unable to defend himself any longer, he was forced to drop to his knees in a frenzied scramble along the nearby ground in search of any abandoned magazines or M16 rifles dropped by other fallen Marines so that he, too, might live.

It wasn't an easy thing to do as much of the area of ground in which he found himself was now stained in dark crimson, with the precious life blood of so many of the dead and wounded – that of the Marines and NVA alike – seemingly strewn everywhere.

"Corpsman up!" was the horrible cry heard too often this day, signaling that an American had been hit and was in need of immediate medical attention.

Often called "Doc" because of the life-saving care they provide on the battlefield, corpsmen are U.S. Navy personnel who have been assigned to Marine combat units. Marines understandably view them as one of their own.

They stayed busy on that unforgettable afternoon in the Que Son Valley.

The images from the widespread carnage will be forever seared into the memories of those who survived. The dead bodies soon became more like those of animals as more time passed in the glare of the unforgiving heat, as most of the soldiers had immediately defecated upon their deaths after losing all muscle control. The pungent smell of feces, gunpowder and blood coated the air like a wet blanket, giving an ugly face to the unmistakable horror of war.

Anticipating being completely overrun any minute by a final wave of enemy forces, Brackeen had given the order from within the bomb crater for his Marines to fix bayonets.

Things had become that dire as the crack NVA soldiers continued their advance, ominously clad in their ubiquitous olive green uniforms and copious layers of tree twigs for camouflage.

"There was no coherent army," MacNichol recalled. "They were just everywhere."

It was now readily apparent the large NVA force incorrectly alleged by U.S. military intelligence to have retreated into the hills and melted into smaller, less lethal units after the fight of two days earlier had instead orchestrated a carefully-prepared trap for the Marines.

And the unsuspecting Americans from Bravo Company had walked right into it.

"We looked up and saw many NVA in full uniforms, packs and cartridge belts running across the rice paddy at us," Hinshaw said. "We started shooting and we could see them falling, but they didn't stop and more and more of them kept coming. Nothing could stop them, and it was like they were doped up."

The inescapable feelings of impending doom grew by the minute among the stunned Americans.

"It was so palpable you were afraid to even breathe," Petrous said. "You felt like they were all around you."

It looked bleak for the Bravo Company Marines.

"We couldn't stop 'em," Brackeen said. "There were too many of them. There was a regiment of them. They just kept coming."

Raymond Pistol was incredulous as he stood quietly and watched the battle rage from his vantage point above the valley back at the Marine combat base on Hill 51. The young Lance

Corporal from Charlie Company was torn with conflicting emotions as the ground below him consistently rattled with violent explosions amidst the deafening sounds of anti-aircraft artillery (AAA) and 50-caliber machine gun rounds, not to mention the pervasive exchange of red and green tracer fire reverberating back and forth through the air.

"My first thought was, 'Thank God, I'm not there,' " he admitted. "But I could see my fellow Marines and friends were catching hell."

Pistol and the other Marines of Charlie Company could only watch in stunned silence as Marine jets repeatedly screamed into the valley, lowering their noses before unleashing their deadly payloads of napalm and 500-pound bombs in support. The ensuing fiery infernos were soon followed by large plumes of black smoke billowing up to the sky as the jets kicked in their after-burners and quickly regained altitude.

It was gut-wrenching for the men of Charlie Company to watch helplessly from the sidelines, but those Marines had been chewed up pretty good themselves as the point company in a previous operation. The company had been assigned security duty at the base as it rebuilt from its own heavy losses with new men and supplies. Those duties included consistently running patrols around the base and catching any small enemy units that might have tried to use the confusion of the ongoing battle to slip away and do damage at the base.

But that was of little immediate use to the embattled men of Bravo Company, who were unable to stem the furious NVA assault despite having already beaten back several waves of enemy soldiers.

"I was so scared I could hardly think," Hinshaw said.

It wasn't long before Brackeen had carefully made his way up from the crater and slid into the trench at Davis' immediate left. He was standing shoulder-to-shoulder with Davis in the trench as 2nd Platoon and the rest of Bravo Company desperately fought for its very survival. Posey was then some several feet away, standing about seven or eight feet left of Davis. There were three Marines right of Davis in the trench, beginning with Leedom at his immediate right and followed by Crandall and Hinshaw.

Young and impetuous, Hinshaw hadn't always been renowned among his comrades-in-arms as a crack Marine. He'd been known to often indulge himself in an array of various worldly delights, prompting more than a few Marines with whom he served to openly question his steadfast dedication and professionalism.

Hinshaw had always been considered by just about everybody in the company to be a very nice kid who was always eager to talk. However, his youthful nonchalance and general inattention to small details while on duty had quickly drawn the ire of both his commanding officers and NCOs alike. As a result, he often drew the unenviable task of latrine outhouse duty as both a stern punishment and a strong incentive to do better. More affectionately referred to as "the burning shitters detail," it entailed having to drag out the many large tubs of the putrid-smelling excrement collected underneath the latrine before dumping kerosene in it, lighting it up and then stirring with a long wooden stick until it turned to ash.

But whatever his prior mistakes, Hinshaw rose to the occasion when the situation called for him to do so that fateful day in the Que Son Valley. He fought courageously in the tactically important corner breach between the trench the Marines occupied and the woods, staving off enemy attempts to flank his platoon despite having been shot twice.

But the roughly 200 or so Marines had already paid a steep price for refusing to yield to a considerably larger enemy force estimated to have been about 2,500. Most notably, one of 2nd Platoon's squad leaders, Lance Corporal Robert Sadler, had been killed a little while earlier after refusing to get into the trench and, instead, choosing to run back and forth to help direct fire.

Sadler had been bravely exhorting his fellow Marines to stand up to the mass of enemy soldiers headed their way before being struck down. His bone-chilling cries of *"They'll kill you if you don't fight back! You must get your heads up and fight! They'll kill you!"* likely gave each Marine reason for at least momentary pause and a clear idea of the dire consequences ahead if they didn't stand up to their oncoming enemy.

It's unlikely Sadler felt anything at all when he took a round in the neck just moments later, his body immediately crumpling to the earth.

His corpse was now one of many littering the ground, while many other Marines were badly wounded.

Yet they continued to persevere in the face of the overwhelming odds.

"I know I was scared shitless," Posey said. "You can't see a man three feet from you get hit in the stomach with two shots and not react with fear. But you try to do something – anything – and hope it's the right thing to do. Get someone to take care of the shot man and try to spot the shooter. See where the grenades are coming from and send a few in return.

"You can't just sit – you have to do."

Added Hinshaw: "I was firing and loading, and firing and loading at the same time."

It wasn't long, however, before the NVA's sheer volume of soldiers had enabled them to creep close enough to easily be within hand grenade range from the thick cover provided in the form of the woods about 20 yards away.

Close enough that the terrified Marines from 2nd Platoon could readily make out the distinct details of the faces of their enemy, even hearing their individual voices as they inched ever forward.

"Sometimes the wall of fire was so great that we couldn't even stand up and fire back," Hinshaw said. "I would just stick my rifle up in the air and fire in the direction from which I knew they were coming."

The NVA immediately began tossing grenades in 2nd Platoon's direction, leaving Davis and the other Marines to instantly react when one would land in the trench at their feet. It made for a surreal scene of sorts as the Marines in immediate harm's way of the deadly bombs would momentarily jump out to escape the subsequent blast before a further barrage of enemy small arms, mortar and machine gun fire would send them scurrying back into the trench for cover.

"You just piled your ass out of [the trench] and let it go off," Brackeen said. "Then you piled back in."

Such a scenario would play out several times over the next half hour like a well-choreographed, wordless ballet with its various ebbs and flows, Brackeen would say later, as the battle raged and both sides sought advantage.

Ironically, the deadly grenades being tossed at the Marines were of American origin, agreed Brackeen, Drollinger and Hinshaw. Other Marines present that day, however, insist that they were Chinese communist grenades.

Either way, the NVA and Viet Cong frequently used weapons captured from U.S., ARVN or other Allied forces, and they much preferred the M26 fragmentation hand grenade and its superior blast range over its Chinese and Russian counterparts in the RGD 33 and the RGD 5, respectively.

Used in close combat to supplement small arms fire against an enemy, the M26 was the grenade of choice for U.S. military forces during the Vietnam War. So the Marines knew from their own training that the grenades being hurled their way were set to explode anywhere from four to six seconds after the pin was pulled and the handle released, and that their lethal fragments exploded up in the air and outward up to about 50 feet to best maximize casualties.

What they didn't know was when the pin had been pulled or how long they had to react after the grenades had initially landed at their feet. So they understandably began piling out of the trench at the first sign of any grenade.

Their good fortune, however, would soon run out when two grenades came their way almost simultaneously. The first sailed high over the trench and exploded harmlessly behind the Marines, but it had succeeded in forcing them to lower their heads and momentarily lose sight of the second incoming shell.

That critical second provided the small opening disaster needed.

"There was one loose in there somewhere, that's all I knew," Brackeen recalled. "I knew that because I saw it coming.

"I had lost track [of the other grenade]. I didn't know where the hell it was. I had already begun shielding my own body."

Unbeknownst to the other Marines desperately fighting for their lives in the trench, the second grenade had suddenly caromed off Hinshaw's leg as he had begun making his way out of the trench and had fallen at all their feet.

Incoming NVA fire and his own frantic efforts to direct his men to throw their own grenades meant that Posey didn't actually see either of the two grenades tossed their way, especially the one that had suddenly ended up just a few short feet to his right.

"I just heard the sound of the grenade landing in the trench," he said. "I heard the 'thump.' It was ... an absolute un-normal sound in that situation."

It was a sound that Posey won't soon forget.

"It just wasn't a right sound," he said. "It gets your attention because with all the weird sounds going on, it was something else that gets your attention. It just made a thud. Everybody was screaming, everybody was shooting. There was incoming and outgoing fire, but that was an absolutely unnatural sound in that situation."

What happened next would indelibly link Davis and his comrades-in-arms while forever etching him into Marine lore.

Nobody will ever know for sure what thoughts were racing through Davis' mind the moment his eyes first spied the grenade. We can only assume that he was acutely aware that several of his fellow Marines such as Posey and Brackeen were still oblivious to the immediate danger lying just at their feet.

We can do so because witnesses later testified that they saw Davis intentionally lunge atop the grenade before using both hands to completely stuff it under his own body, making certain he absorbed the entire lethal blast.

The cast iron grenade and its deadly filling of TNT suddenly went off with a fury, violently launching his body several feet into the air and killing him instantly. Davis' lifeless corpse then crashed back down to the ground at roughly 5 p.m. local time.

He never made a sound while sacrificing his own life for his fellow Marines without the slightest hesitation.

"I saw that grenade land," Leedom said. "I turned my back, went the other way [out of the trench] and the next thing I knew, I heard a thud. There was nothing else."

"I didn't know who it was at first," Posey said. "Then I saw it was Rodney. I didn't know it was him before that. He'd thrown himself – he'd come down onto the grenade – and was pushing it to get it further under him.

"He was facing me, probably about seven or eight feet away. [The grenade] went off and he flew into the air. He turned in the air and landed on the edge of the trench on his back. I could see his whole chest was ripped open. Then he slid down into the bottom of the trench."

Drollinger was also under heavy fire from the oncoming enemy force, but he and Petrous were among the other Marines close enough to witness the heroic action.

"He pulled [the grenade] in," Drollinger said of Davis. "He knew what he was doing. There's no ifs, ands or buts about it."

The intense fighting continued following Davis' death, but a wounded Brackeen soon ordered his Marines to pull back yet again to better consolidate their position until help arrived. He'd been hit in the left hand about 20 minutes after Davis had been killed, and likely would have died himself if the notebook he was carrying in the shirt pocket of his government-issued green fatigues hadn't somehow stopped a bullet intended for him.

But Brackeen had recognized the need for his platoon to immediately withdraw back to a tree line along the edge of the village.

The Marines quickly rounded up all of their wounded, leaving their dead behind for the time being before making their way back the more than 160 feet or so back under the cover of teargas and setting up a new defensive perimeter.

"We've got to pull back!" Brackeen screamed to his men. "We've got no choice. We've got to pull back."

The decision to even temporarily leave their fallen behind was a difficult one, and reached only out of necessity. Marines have long been ingrained from early on to never leave another man behind under any circumstances. Brackeen, however, took small solace in knowing his troops would still be able to effectively protect their bodies with rifle fire from their new position.

The heavy fighting continued unabated for about another half hour before finally subsiding, thanks in some large part to some timely jet and artillery-delivered teargas strikes that helped keep the NVA at bay while also preventing reinforcements from joining their ranks. Things had become so dicey that the supporting Marine jets had been forced to drop their powerful 500-pound bombs within 150 feet of the new Marine perimeter.

Posey felt his own death was imminent as well.

"I remember someone moved down the line from the corner on the right, towards the left," he said. "It could have been Hinshaw or Leedom or the Lieutenant.

"When he stopped, I told him, 'If I get hit and die, take my watch and other stuff. Don't let the NVA take it!' "

The enemy attack soon began to waver, however, and shooting erupted only periodically the rest of the evening.

The day's combat operations were officially declared over at 1 a.m. on the morning of Sept. 7, some eight hours or so after an isolated Bravo Company first came under fire, according to the Combat After Action Report. During that violent span, 35 Marines had lost their lives, while 92 others had been wounded, many seriously. More than 100 NVA soldiers were killed and scores more seriously wounded during that particular day's battle, according to U.S. military figures.

Operation Swift would last another nine days. By the time it finally concluded on Sept. 15, the NVA had largely ceded control of the southern half of the Que Son Valley to the Americans. The area remained relatively quiet from that point until the Marines turned the region over to the U.S. Army a few weeks later.

****

U.S. intelligence agencies later determined that the two regiments from the NVA's 2nd Division most active during Operation Swift had been rendered unfit for combat. The heavy losses sustained by the North Vietnamese in the Que Son Valley likely played a role in assuring that nearby Da Nang didn't join South Vietnam's many other major cities that were initially overwhelmed a few months later during the Tet Offensive of 1968.

But the victory had been a Pyrrhic one.

All the Marines who had been in the trench with Davis were in agreement that his action had saved their lives and had played a critical role in saving the day against the enemy advance.

It would be a long time before either Posey, Leedom or Brackeen could get over consistently dwelling on what had transpired that unforgettable day, and how it was that their own lives had been spared. Or how one selfless act of heroism at one critical moment had not only indelibly altered their own individual life path trajectories, but that of their own immediate families as well.

"He took the entire blast," Posey added later. "There was nothing that came out. I know I was close enough that I would have been seriously hurt or perhaps killed if any blast had escaped.

"I have often wondered if I could do the same. I don't know. I suppose you only find out at that instant."

Brackeen had likewise wrestled for a long time with what had transpired before finally coming to terms with the fact that he was alive only because of Davis.

"Why he made that decision I'll never know," he said. "I'll never know. I'll go to my grave not knowing. He did a very heroic thing."

But an eternally grateful and appreciative Brackeen would also admit to later wondering about the wisdom of somebody of Davis' stature within the military hierarchy committing such a gallant, yet sacrificial act.

"Like it or not," he said, "[Davis] was third-in-command of the platoon."

What he didn't understand at the time was that Davis had been raised to do nothing less. He'd always taken it upon himself while growing up to always look out after those closest to him and others in need of help. He never had a thought of doing otherwise.

Not even in Vietnam.

It wasn't until later on the morning of Sept. 7 that Davis' remains and those of the other fallen Marines were recovered. Lined up on ponchos along the ground, the bodies of the dead – black and white – had already begun bloating and all looking very much alike after extended time in the searing heat and humidity, their natural skin tones having given way to an ashen, almost gray façade as rigor mortis had begun to set in. The differences in the texture of their hair was then about only way to distinguish each man's race.

There were 48 Marines assigned to 2nd Platoon when it left its combat base on Hill 51 on the early morning of Sept. 4, including a two-man sniper team, two machine gunners and a forward artillery observer.

By the time the battered platoon managed to finally return on Sept. 8, that number had dwindled to a mere 11. The rest had either been killed or wounded seriously enough to warrant immediate evacuation to a hospital.

Of the 11 remaining platoon members still capable of fighting, eight would later receive Purple Hearts for bullet and grenade fragment wounds suffered during combat in Operation Swift.

CHAPTER 10

THE IMMEDIATE AFTERMATH

A convoy of medevac helicopters began arriving on station on the morning of Sept. 7, first ferrying out the scores of Marine wounded before beginning to load the dead aboard. It was Leedom who solemnly carried Davis' remains out to an awaiting chopper later that morning to begin his final journey home.

"He saved my ass," an emotional Leedom reflected. "He saved my life, and there's not a day that goes by when I don't think about Sgt. Davis."

All of the American dead and wounded had been flown out by noon.

The few men still left in Bravo Company, 2nd Platoon spent the day consolidating their lines, trying to account for everybody following the chaos of Sept. 6th and rounding up all the decaying bodies from both sides. Abandoned weapons and discarded combat gear were strewn all over the place from the lengthy pitched battle from the day before and also had to be collected.

Meanwhile, resupply operations were ongoing throughout the day, as the Marines were almost entirely devoid of nearly all ammunition, but especially grenades. They were also in dire need of additional food and water.

While all that was going on, engineers were busy gathering up the extremely large amounts of captured enemy ammunition, mortar rounds, rocket propelled grenades and other explosives. The weapons were tossed into various wells, where the captured ordnance was quickly primed with C-4 plastic explosives and blown up so as to never be used again.

The weary Marines loved the engineers because they could always count on begging or borrowing enough small amounts of C-4 from them to use to boil water with or to heat their C-rations. But, first and foremost, the Marines enjoyed the kind of illuminating fireworks show that came when the engineers blew things up. This one came at an especially good time as the Marines were desperately looking for something to at least briefly take their minds off the horror of the previous day's savage combat and their many losses from it.

It was just a momentary escape, but one that came as soothing relief nonetheless to sleep- and food-deprived Marines worn down by the kind of intense carnage to which they'd been subject over two of the previous three days.

Bravo Company eventually limped back to base at Hill 51 on Sept. 8, using the next week or so to incorporate the many new men it had been sent as replacements. That included a permanent one for Reese, who would never be the same after that fateful day. He would spend a lengthy period in the hospital while recovering from his severe wounds before being killed in a car accident in the Washington, D.C. area many years later.

Lieutenant Ken Vitucci had assumed command of 2nd Platoon as the wounded Brackeen began his convalescence from his injuries in a hospital in Japan. Bravo Company was assigned perimeter duty back at the base while it struggled to get back up to full strength.

The remainder of Operation Swift was relatively quiet with the Marines having no major contact with the enemy.

The remainder of 1967 continued to be an aggressive combat period, as the Marines pulling duty in the Que Son Valley continued to regularly comb the area with platoon-sized sweeps in the bush. It became commonplace during that time to run into small groups of as many as 10 Viet Cong at a time, but it wouldn't be until the Tet Offensive of January 1968 that the Marines would encounter any more large-scale engagements with enemy forces like that seen during Operation Swift.

President Lyndon B. Johnson later recognized the First Marine Division with a Presidential Unit Citation, citing the Marines' *"extraordinary heroism and outstanding performance of duty in action against the North Vietnamese Army and Viet Cong forces in the Republic of Vietnam, from 29 March 1966 to September 1967."*

CHAPTER 11

BREAKING THE NEWS

It had been a quiet night, with everybody sleeping soundly throughout the Davis residence in Macon when the shrill screams began and awoke all in the house.

Judy Davis' terrifying dream was an indelible image no wife ever wanted to see, and it had appeared disturbingly real to her. Her prophetic vision of her husband lying dead in his own pool of blood had suddenly shaken her from her peaceful slumber, rendering her a quivering mess. Family members desperately tried their best to console her, assure her somehow that Rodney was indeed OK.

It took some time, but Judy eventually calmed down and everybody went back to sleep.

The incident, however, proved to be a chilling harbinger of the entire family's nightmare-come-true that began the very next day as official word arrived that Rodney had indeed been killed in Vietnam a few days earlier.

The two uniformed Marines charged to personally deliver the stark news were still outside, barely out of the standard government-issued car they were driving when their approach was first spotted at about noon. They had just begun making their way up the steps towards the front door of the Davis home when

Judy Davis' eye caught their movements through the glass door from where she stood in the kitchen.

She immediately froze in her tracks, even as the Marines moved closer still.

And with ample reason, too. It was the one sight any family with loved ones serving in the military never wants to see because it meant the unimaginable had taken place. The Marines charged with that solemn duty were the unambiguous messengers of death.

Suddenly overwhelmed with grief, Judy Davis promptly fainted and collapsed to the floor.

Family members at the house at the time immediately rushed to her side and tended to the new widow.

"Oh, no, no, no!" Judy screamed aloud after gathering herself. "Not Rodney! Not Rodney! Not my Rodney!"

The Marines only confirmed that Rodney had been killed in action by an enemy grenade a few days earlier and that his body had since been taken to the Marine mortuary in Da Nang in preparation for its return home for burial.

Because not all the facts were yet in, there was no mention whatsoever at the time of the unique circumstances surrounding his death. Or that an investigation was soon forthcoming that would eventually lead to his posthumously being awarded the Medal of Honor.

Word of Davis' death soon spread, as the rest of the Davis family and their many friends came together to begin the family's grieving period. Then a college student at nearby Fort Valley State University, Howard Davis happened to be at home at the time the news was delivered and took it upon himself to contact his parents and his oldest brother Gordon.

But Gordon Davis had already endured a strange premonition of his own, and had begun suspecting some time earlier that misfortune had come to his beloved brother long before the phone rang at his home in Albany to confirm his worst fears.

That's because he knew the kind of man his brother was.

"Rodney might have treated you like a dog, but he wouldn't have left you anywhere," Gordon Davis said. "That's how he got killed – not leaving folks. He didn't have any damn business there – he should have got the hell out of Dodge. But he didn't leave folks - he was that kind of guy.

"If he was with you, he was with you for keeps."

It wasn't long before Robert Davis, then a high school freshman, soon arrived back at the family home, as did Debra, who was but just a middle school student at the time. Debra had been pulled from class and given a ride home by compassionate school officials, although she hadn't initially guessed as to the reason why. She knew immediately, however, something was amiss as they neared the Davis family home and she began to spy the phalanx of visitors' cars that had already begun gathering along the street outside.

Granny soon returned home from the typing class she was taking at the time, with Gordon Davis, Sr. following suit shortly later after word of his son's tragic death in Vietnam reached him at a nearby construction site.

The family was devastated by the news and consoled one another the best they could under the trying circumstances.

The Davis family soon began receiving condolences from all over for their loss, but perhaps none were as personally heartfelt as that from Brackeen. Only alive because of his action, Rodney Davis' former commanding officer had penned a letter from his own hospital room in Japan to Davis' widow, lauding her late husband for *"fighting for a cause he believed in."*

"Dear Mrs. Davis," the wounded lieutenant wrote in a letter dated Sept. 14, 1967.

"I realize there isn't much I can say to relieve your grief at the loss of your husband, Rodney.

Although I served with Rodney only a short time, I had already recognized his courage and selflessness. He was very respected by all the men in the platoon.

His loss was a blow to us all, and the absence of so great a man has left an unfillable spot in our ranks and in our hearts.

I think Rodney died fighting for a cause he believed in.

If I can be of any assistance to you whatsoever, please do not hesitate to write me. God bless you during this darkest of hours.

Sincerely,

Lt. John Brackeen"

Davis' remains arrived in Macon on Sept. 20, 1967, escorted on the long trip home by Marine Sgt. Franklin E. Heard.

Despite their overwhelming grief, there were still some in the family who held out a sliver of hope that there had been a huge mistake, that maybe it was someone else who had been killed and not their beloved son, husband, brother and close friend.

Vietnam was on the other side of the world, thousands of miles away from Macon, so the family just had to be certain when the body finally returned home and had been picked up by the local funeral home located not far from the Davis residence.

They had all heard the day's many outlandish stories that were making the rounds in support of the alleged cases of mistaken identity, not to mention the many tall tales of empty military caskets coming back to the United States, or sometimes with just sand or tires inside instead of the body of a fallen American serviceman.

They had to know for sure themselves, so Gordon Davis, Sr. and his oldest son and namesake went to the funeral home to view the body and make certain on behalf of the entire family. As his father and the head of the household, Gordon Davis, Sr. understandably felt the somber duty was his to do. His eldest son insisted on coming along with him because he knew that he needed to see the body of his beloved brother and best friend for his own closure.

"I had to see for myself," Gordon Davis said.

Their worst fears were soon confirmed – Rodney M. Davis was gone. He was among Macon's staggering total of 56 sons to lose their lives in Vietnam.

Davis was buried at the family plot at Linwood Cemetery in Macon on Sept. 23, 1967 and currently rests there alongside both of his parents as the storied graveyard's most celebrated hero yet.

CHAPTER 12

CONTEXTUALIZING DAVIS' DEATH

Davis' death in Vietnam in 1967 had come during one of the most volatile social periods in U.S. history, as the nation was racked with domestic strife from the ongoing Civil Rights and Anti-War movements.

America suddenly appeared to be on the verge of coming apart at the seams as a result, with many of its citizens now finding themselves pitted against one another during what was easily one of the country's most polarized domestic climates ever.

Those rising racial tensions would first begin coming to a precarious head in 1967, combining the pent-up frustrations borne the lack of real racial equality, economic disparity, bitter disdain for the war and other pivotal events of the day to form the perfect storm for chaos and lawlessness.

But strains had been boiling to a crescendo all across the country in prior years as African-Americans tired of being denied basic civil rights had begun standing up in peaceful, but defiant protests all over the nation, often in the face of the threat of violence. Their patience eventually wore out as progress towards full equality had been painstakingly slow in coming.

It was just a matter of time before America's long simmering powder keg of black and white finally exploded into ugly violence.

It threatened to tear the country apart when it finally did during the long, hot summer of 1967.

Activist Robert L. Allen eventually would later characterize the tumultuous year as *"an important turning point in the history of black America. It was a year of unprecidentally massive and widespread urban revolts. It was the year that so-called riots became an institutionalized form of black protest."*

Frustrated African-Americans had finally begun lashing out with violence across some of America's biggest cities in their demand to be heard.

It was on April 19, 1967, that Stokely Carmichael, the leader of the Student Nonviolent Coordinating Committee (SNCC), first coined the phrase "black power" in a speech in Seattle. He defined the term as *"the coming together of black people to fight for their liberation by any means necessary."*

Long defined by intolerance and bigotry, the longstanding tensions between the races had only been further exacerbated by the growing discontent over the war in Vietnam. The war had expanded following a massive American military build-up at the start of the year and the decision to include offensive operations on North Vietnamese targets. By the end of 1967, there would be nearly half a million U.S. troops in Vietnam.

As the war escalated, so, too, did American casualties and fierce opposition to the conflict.

Tensions were running high everywhere, and it wasn't long before the hot-button issue of race and its manifestation within the military had become inextricably intertwined.

And equally as controversial.

In the times leading up to the Vietnam War, African-Americans had often tended to view military service very favorably, as a place that usually offered more opportunities than many of their own hometowns. Many African-Americans such as Rodney M. Davis joined the armed forces right out of high school so as to receive the kind of training, career opportunities and wages that were routinely being denied to them in the civilian world due to widespread racism throughout America, but particularly in the South in places like Macon.

Given the dearth of equal opportunities available at the time in most other U.S. institutions, the military became one of the few places where African-Americans would feel they could at least expect somewhat of a fair shake.

Even that wasn't always the case, but they nevertheless deeply loved their country despite its faults, and relished the chance to serve. Patriotism knows no colors.

That's why Dan Bullock, an African-American from Brooklyn, N.Y., so readily lied about his age so as to enlist in the Marine Corps. He was a 15-year-old private first class when he was killed in action during a firefight at the An Hoa Combat Base in the Quang Nam Province on June 7, 1969, making him the youngest American serviceman to die in Vietnam.

African-Americans have historically fought as bravely and as heroically alongside white Americans, but have typically done so without any fanfare. Hollywood, for the most part, has never rushed to embrace their many accomplishments, as it has so readily done in the past for other equally-as-worthy valiant white soldiers such as Sgt. Alvin York from World War I and decorated World War II heroes such as Audie Murphy and famed Marine ace fighter pilot Greg "Pappy" Boyington.

Yet, the achievements of Davis and other African-American soldiers are perhaps all the more laudable, given the fact they accomplished as much in the face of institutionalized racism and discrimination.

It takes a special man with a unique devotion to his country to defend it even though it has denied him full rights as a citizen. It takes an even more extraordinary one still to willingly give his life for that country.

But the question of why Davis or any other African-American would ever choose to still make such a sacrifice and why other soldiers of color would do likewise for a country that often treated them like pariahs at home underscores both the paradox and unique challenges America's wars have always posed for African-Americans.

It has been a long-running debate among many African-Americans over their rightful place in their country's society and how to best reach that goal. African-Americans have been a people who have lived in this country for the longest time with little hope of ever fully sharing in the American Dream. So, while terrible, the sound of combat has also heralded renewed expectations of newfound social and economic opportunities and of someday perhaps being fully included in the mainstream as an active participant in political and civic life once the shooting stopped.

It was during the Civil War that Frederick Douglass first began advocating black participation in combat units as some sort of proof of black courage and manhood. Douglass had hoped such a strong show of patriotism would elicit at least a grudging acceptance from whites back home and expedite the assimilation of blacks into the mainstream culture.

Noted scholar W.E.B. Du Bois would preach similarly in World War I, but not all black civil rights leaders were on board with such thinking. It was in helping to persuade President Harry Truman to end segregation within the military in 1948 that A. Phillip Randolph pointed out that African-Americans had previously fought in all of their country's wars, dating back to the Revolution, only to still be denied full citizenship.

But all of that was merely intangible philosophy to be debated later by others. None of it certainly mattered to Rodney M. Davis during the daily life-and-death struggles in which he had suddenly found himself immersed in Vietnam.

He'd always been raised to do right by people, to help others less fortunate or capable of doing for themselves.

Black, white or any other color.

He had done as much for his four siblings while growing up in Macon under Jim Crow. He was determined to do no less for his new brothers in the Marine Corps also in harm's way. Unquestioned loyalty to those closest to him had always been one of Davis' strongest virtues.

It was always that simple for him, but President Lyndon B. Johnson enjoyed no such luxury.

The need for more men to fight the war in Vietnam forced Johnson to announce on March 6, 1967 his plan to establish a draft lottery. The problem was that draft boards that determined which young men were called into service and likely headed to the meat grinder of southeast Asia were overwhelmingly white in almost every case. In 1967, there were no African-Americans represented on the boards in Alabama, Arkansas, Mississippi or Louisiana.

In fact, one draft board member in Louisiana was an unrepentant Grand Wizard in the Ku Klux Klan. Jack Helms even went as far as to publicly label the NAACP as *"a communist-inspired, anti-Christ, sex-perverted group of tennis short beatniks."*

Selective Service regulations at the time offered deferments for college attendance and a variety of other essential civilian occupations, all of which favored middle- and upper-class whites as the draftees were typically poor, undereducated and blue-collar workers. Even just the consideration of opening the draft to all college students was considered political suicide. Coveted spots in state National Guard units were another way to avoid service in Vietnam, but they were equally as dominated with whites from wealthy families with deep political connections.

The destructive impact of the draft was therefore considerably greater within the African-American community. Not surprisingly, it wasn't long before wild rumors began spreading among the most easily led that the U.S. government was using the Vietnam War as a sort of genocide.

Many civil right leaders often noted the indisputable fact that the growing war was draining large amounts of money from President Johnson's "Great Society" program that might have otherwise eased the impoverished conditions in many of American's urban communities, most of which were black and extremely poor.

Black Panther leader Eldridge Cleaver had voiced his strong opinion to the contradictory situation, declaring in a speech that *"black Americans are asked to die for the system in Vietnam; in Watts (a poor black suburb of Los Angeles) they are asked to die by it."*

Dr. Martin Luther King, Jr. had already begun expressing his concerns about the war and the way it was being run by the time he first morally equated the Civil Rights movement he led to the growing opposition of the Vietnam War in January 1967. He said he supported the anti-war movement on ethical grounds, citing the war's draining of valuable resources that could be better used at home and the higher percentage of African-American casualties in relation to the total population.

King was in New York City when he made his most widely-known and most comprehensive statement against the war on April 4, 1967. Speaking to a crowd of 3,000 people at Riverside Church, he delivered a speech entitled "Beyond Vietnam: A Time to Break Silence." In that discourse, King charged that the expanding war effort was *"taking the black young men who had been crippled by our society and sending them eight thousand miles away to guarantee liberties in Southeast Asia which they had not found in southwest Georgia and East Harlem. So we have been repeatedly faced with the cruel irony of watching Negro and white boys on TV screens as they kill and die together for a nation that has been unable to sit them together in the same schools. So we watch them in brutal solidarity burning the huts of a poor village, but we realize that they would never live together on the same block in Detroit."*

The recipient of the 1964 Nobel Peace Prize, King would eventually call Vietnam *"one of the most unjust wars that has ever been fought in the history of the world"* and would further describe the growing conflict in Southeast Asia as *"a white man's war, a black man's fight."*

Adding to the tensions was the April 1967 arrest of colorful world heavyweight boxing champion Muhammad Ali for draft evasion. Ali had been denied conscientious objector status and refused to join the Army.

"I ain't got no quarrel with the Viet Cong ... No Viet Cong ever called me nigger," he had famously declared a few months earlier.

The Vietnam War may have been the match that ignited the combustible social inferno threatening the nation, but the sensitive issue of race was clearly the kindling where it all began.

Three years after the passing of the landmark Civil Rights Act of 1964, Jim Crow laws were still prevalent in many places throughout the South, denying African-Americans their full rights in cities like Davis' hometown of Macon, Georgia and elsewhere.

Other events of the day also played a role in America's venomous state of race relations in 1967.

The U.S. Supreme Court's landmark ruling in *Loving vs. Virginia* on June 12, 1967 decreed the prohibiting of interracial marriage to be unconstitutional. The case centered around Mildred Loving, a black woman, and Richard Loving, a white man, the couple who had been sentenced to a year in prison in Virginia for marrying one another.

Their marriage violated Virginia's anti-miscegenation statute, the Racial Integrity Act of 1924 that prohibited marriages between people classified as "white" and those classified as "colored."

The Supreme Court's unanimous decision in declaring the law unconstitutional on grounds that it violated the Equal Protection Clause of the 14th Amendment forced the 16 states that still had such statutes on the books forbidding such a union to void them. The high court's decision came at a time when polls showed that 70 percent of Americans were against marriage equality for interracial couples.

Further antagonizing those who sought to impede America's ongoing progress in racial relations was President Johnson's historic announcement the following day on June 13 that he was nominating Thurgood Marshall to succeed the retiring justice Tom Clark of Texas and become the first African-American to sit on the Supreme Court.

Marshall was confirmed by the U.S. Senate on Aug. 30, and formally sworn in as an associate justice of the nation's highest court on Oct. 2, 1967, where he would stay for the next 24 years. During the floor vote, Johnson had used the considerable influence he had escrowed from his many years in Congress, including a six-year stint as the Senate Majority Leader, to convince 20 Senators *not* to vote on the matter. Virtually every Southern senator voted against Marshall's confirmation, including Herman Talmadge, Georgia's own unrepentant segregationist.

The feelings of frustration, anger and powerlessness in the face of overt racism, high rates of unemployment, poverty, police brutality and inadequate public services among African-Americans had built to a crescendo. They collectively led to the race riots in the summer of 1967 in more than 150 cities across the country, including Newark, Detroit, New York City, Cleveland, Tampa, Hartford, Boston, Washington, D.C., Chicago, Nashville, Milwaukee, Memphis and Durham, N.C. among others.

Violence, as H. Rap Brown had so famously decreed, had seemingly become *"as American as cherry pie."*

The brutality of what was happening stateside and the indelible images of armed American soldiers standing ready at the trigger on our nation's own streets proved just as shocking as the events going on thousands of miles away in Vietnam and only further polarized the nation, both politically and socially.

Macon had managed to avoid the violence at least at that time, although tensions were running extremely high. Long considered the cradle to the civil rights movement, nearby Atlanta, the city that ironically called itself too busy to hate, had already endured its own race riot a few months earlier in early September 1966.

A proud segregationist, Georgia Governor Lester Maddox attributed the riots to *"a communist conspiracy."*

An 11-member body charged in the immediate aftermath to study the origins of the destructive riots, the National Advisory Commission on Civil Disorders berated the federal and state governments for failed housing, education and social service policies. The investigative body, which was better known as the Kerner Commission, concluded the United States was *"moving towards two societies, one black, one white – separate and unequal."*

America was now closer to anarchy than at any point since the Civil War.

The Kerner Commission saved some criticism for the mainstream media, saying its occasional exaggeration of events and bias in looking at things from only the view of white men only further fanned the flames of discontent among African-Americans and white Americans alike. The panel called on the news media to diversify its ranks, and to begin committing resources to covering black communities on a regular basis.

Perhaps nowhere was the point of the white-dominated news media's insensitivity more readily apparent than in the contrast between Davis' obituary that ran in the Macon Telegraph on Sept. 15, 1967 and one that just two days earlier detailed the death of a young, white second lieutenant from Macon also killed while serving in Vietnam.

Davis' obituary of a mere couple of lines was unceremoniously listed on page 16, easily lost in the middle of the

10 death and funeral notices that ran that day. Only his family and close friends specifically looking for the notice would have ever seen it.

Conversely, the detailed story of two days earlier that chronicled the combat-related death in Vietnam of 21-year-old white Macon native Bricey Elrod Lamb was prominently featured as a separate news story splashed in the middle of the paper's front page.

Davis' death would later become front-page local news, but only after it was learned that he could possibly become Macon's first Medal of Honor recipient.

Likewise, a later March 27, 1969 Chicago Tribune story that detailed Davis' heroism that had led to his being posthumously awarded the Medal of Honor at the White House just the day before. In the article's lead paragraph, the writer flippantly referred to Davis as a "Negro marine sergeant from Georgia."

A New York Times account that ran the same day noted that Davis was "the 10th Negro to receive the award for heroism in Vietnam."

Left unstated in either story was the flawed, but socially-accepted and color-coded premise at the time that it was somehow shocking that an African-American soldier would ever be capable of such heroism and courage while under fire. The color of white soldiers also honored for valor was usually never mentioned in the news stories of that era.

CHAPTER 13

BLACK, WHITE AND MARINE GREEN

Why?

Why Rodney Davis lunged atop that grenade at the expense of his own life is the quintessential question that has haunted not only those who stood closest to him at that critical moment, but his own family and friends as well for more than four decades.

Why would a young man with a beautiful young wife and two infant children eagerly awaiting his return home from overseas commit such a noble and courageous, yet sacrificial act? And for white Marines he barely knew? And for a country that often treated him like a second-class citizen at the time?

"It puzzles me to this day," Leedom said. "To save my ass? I just don't know."

Those who have served in the military will readily tell you that nobody plans on being a hero – it just happens. They say they are just ordinary men who do what they do not so much for glory, God or country as much as it is for never wanting to let down the guy next to them.

The contentious issue of race was everywhere in 1967, and it was readily apparent that the issue wasn't going away anytime soon. But the ominous specter of death just around the corner at any minute tended to have a sobering effect on improving race relations.

Or at least it did in a hot, steamy sliver of the world several thousand miles away.

Combat vets from Vietnam say it was much more prevalent for race-related problems to usually arise among rear echelon types or on domestic installations, where people's very lives were not entirely dependent on the men next to them. The military experienced a number of serious race riots at a number of different installations between 1968 and 1973.

The assassination of Dr. Martin Luther King in April 1968 only served to further enflame racial tensions among the troops, as racist graffiti, cross burnings, Confederate flags and Ku Klux Klan materials immediately began appearing on some installations from some white troops.

African-American troops angry at recent events soon began toting "Black Power" symbols as a gesture of their solidarity in the face of perceived institutional oppression. They often pointed out the hypocrisy in the U.S. decision to fight enemies abroad who proclaimed the right to enslave or exterminated allegedly inferior races while subjecting its own minorities back home to discrimination and abuse.

The Viet Cong and NVA sought to take advantage of the growing American racial divide, often leaving various leaflets throughout the jungles for Americans to find showing pictures of U.S. policemen back home brutalizing civil rights workers or the young African-Americans bravely seeking their full rights in the hopes it would lessen the fighting spirit of the American units. The enemy propaganda attempts increased after Dr. Martin Luther King's assassination in 1968 and served to further heighten racial tensions within the American ranks.

The U.S. Navy perhaps experienced the most potentially damaging racial disturbance of them all in October 1972, when a major race riot broke out aboard the aircraft carrier USS Kitty Hawk and threatened combat operations. Forty-six sailors were injured during the melee that involved more than 100 ship personnel as the Kitty Hawk had been steaming to her station in the Gulf of Tonkin off Vietnam's coast.

Among the findings of a subsequent Congressional subcommittee on the racial violence within the military was that *"the average young black man has racial pride, drive for identity and sensitivity to discrimination that is characteristic of the young black in the United States."*

It was soon obvious that racial tensions were also rising within the U.S., and that they didn't stop at the door when those young men entered the military.

Yet, that kind of bitter racial discord was rarely seen on the ground in tense frontline combat zones, veterans say, where daily survival meant entrusting that the man in the foxhole next to you always had your back.

Black or white, rich or poor, Jew or Gentile. Their pedigree didn't matter in the least.

The troops serving together immediately in harm's way often shared canteens and cigarettes, oblivious to their racial differences. They often cried together, laughed together and sadly even died together in one another's arms on far too many other occasions.

They shared same mud, the same blood.

"We all bled red, and we were Marines," Posey said. "You cannot put your life in the hands of someone who detests you. I have no doubt [racism] was an issue somewhere, but a crisis situation will make the biggest idiot get wise fast."

Soldiers have never had the luxury of choosing their comrades in times of conflict – they are assigned to them. Only the present mattered in Vietnam's deadly jungles and soggy rice paddies, where men of varying races, ethnicities, education levels, socio-economic backgrounds and political persuasions all shared the one most basic desire of all.

To survive.

Theirs was an unbreakable bond, an eternal brotherhood that transcended any and all of their many other differences. The rest of America may have been stuck at the time on the divisive issue of black and white, but such polarizing discourse had no place on the dangerous front lines of Vietnam.

As has so often been the case throughout history, necessity is usually the midwife for progress.

"We lived together, and for one another," Brackeen said.

Petrous insists that it didn't matter in the slightest what color the guy was next to him when he and his fellow Marines were out on patrol during Vietnam's rainy monsoon season and forced to withstand their share of drastic temperature drops following each of the many downpours. The frequent sudden outbursts left the Marines wet and shivering after having just been sweating through their fatigues in the extreme heat just a little while earlier.

It was typical for three Marines to occupy each foxhole as they settled in for the night, with any two of them required to be awake at all times to keep watch. Cold, wet and miserable as they followed orders and fulfilled their duty, they had little choice but to huddle closely together to stay warm and retain their body heat in temperatures that had suddenly plummeted to about 60 degrees in a very short period of time.

The color or pedigree of the man beside him keeping him warm made no difference whatsoever to Petrous or any of the other Marines of Bravo Company. Theirs would always be a special relationship, forged by a shared adversity during such trying missions and the ominous spectre of death at any moment.

But the young Marines were hardly oblivious of all the tumultuous happenings back home either. Mail call was always a big hit upon their arrival back from patrols of several days in the bush, immediately buoying their spirits by allowing the war-weary Marines to put aside their constant fatigue and thoughts of the horrors of war so that they could at least temporarily reconnect with friends and family back at home.

The incoming correspondence awaiting the Marines back at base camp not only included much-anticipated letters from home that often detailed all that was happening back in America, but usually also the latest copies of *Stars and Stripes*, the Pentagon-sponsored newspaper for U.S. military personnel whose content was always rigidly screened.

But not even the U.S. military thought it was possible to escape the news of the many events going on back home, so it wisely decided to avoid even trying to do so. As a result, even the sanitized versions of the ugly race riots offered by *Stars and Stripes* were quickly grabbed up and captured the Marines' attention first.

Many of those young Americans either themselves hailed from the cities experiencing the violent social unrest or knew someone who did.

Petrous still recalls the afternoon in late July 1967 when Bravo Company returned to camp and first read of the riots that had befallen both Newark and Detroit. Glad to be done with their patrol and safely back at base, he and fellow Marine Curtis Mitchell, who happened to be African-American, were captivated by what they were reading of the race riots threatening to tear the country asunder.

The two were sharing some oatmeal cookies that Petrous' mother had sent to her son when they first sat down together in their bunker just before dark to go through the Stars and Stripes account of the racial violence and began talking about it. Petrous, who had a particular interest in getting up-to-date with events because he hailed from Detroit, was always quick with a joke.

And this occasion was no different.

"Aren't you glad we're safe over here in Vietnam from all that stuff?" he laughed to his friend. "But don't worry, Mitchell. If we win, I'll buy you."

"If we win, I'll buy you," his friend shot back.

Both men laughed aloud at their little exchange, never for one minute thinking anything less of one another because of exploding racial tensions thousands of miles away back at home in the U.S. Certainly, what was going on back in America was no amusing matter, but the conversation spoke to the special relationship these young Marines had with one another while serving in Vietnam and the inherent deep trust that was the result of putting their lives in one another's hands each and every day.

"We didn't give a shit about that stuff," Petrous recalled. "We just laughed at it and made it go away."

Hilgartner, who relinquished command of the 1/5 shortly following the conclusion of Operation Swift after taking over the battalion in November 1966, recalled a telling story about race relations following a routine patrol prior to Davis' arrival in the summer of 1967.

Hot and bothered after a lengthy march through the steamy jungle with full packs and gear, the Marines were thrilled to come upon the cool water of the Song Ly Ly they often used to bathe.

Aware that his men were hot, tired and filthy after a few days out in the bush, Hilgartner gave the OK for a quick break in the naturally-forming pool that was the result of the river's change in direction from west to south.

Security teams quickly assumed positions all around the area as the young, sweaty Marines wasted no time in disrobing and lunging into the soothing water that ran some five or six feet deep. Hilgartner, who had previously served in the Korean War, had soon joined his troops in the hasty efforts to rid themselves of all the filth they had accumulated on their bodies and manage at least a short reprieve from the energy-sapping heat that often reached well over 100 degrees during the summer, even in the shade.

Things were going smoothly until two corporals – one black, one white – suddenly began fighting in the water after a joke had gone awry. Fists immediately flew and angry words followed, immediately worrying Hilgartner that what began as an innocuous incident might become something much worse if action weren't taken immediately.

Hilgartner, who was nicknamed "Highpockets" by his men because he literally towered well above most of them at 6-foot-6, was still in his boots and only covered by a towel when he jumped into the water, personally grabbed the two startled Marines and immediately began admonishing them. Hilgartner was still wearing his hat showing his rank at the time as a not-so-subtle reminder to his authority, but knew his men were aware of the growing racial divide back home. He sought to make sure from the outset that this episode didn't spiral out of control and lead to the kind of venom that had now become dangerously prevalent thousands of miles away on America's streets.

"We don't have this kind of stuff in our battalion!" he screamed at the two men.

Hilgartner later ordered both young men to report to him later that day. They were unsure what penalty to expect when they finally stood in front of their angry commanding officer, who instructed them to fill 100 sandbags to be used in defense of the base as punishment. Hilgartner's rationale was sound because he knew that the two Marines would have to work together to accomplish their mission or face a reduction in both rank and pay.

Sweaty and exhausted after putting their differences aside long enough to complete their assigned task, the two Marines reported back to Hilgartner, who chided them one more time about the critical importance of getting along.

"Your sentence is suspended," he told them. "Now report to your platoons and remember this: We have only one color in this battalion and it is Marine green. We're fighting a war out here, and it's the enemy we fight, not each other. Is that clear?"

"Yes, sir," both men quickly replied before scurrying off, their lesson learned.

Danger was all around them in the Que Son Valley, so the last thing his Marines needed to be doing was fighting amongst each other. The issue of race, Hilgartner had explained to them, had no place where death was never far away.

"To me, skin color doesn't make a squat of difference," said Hilgartner, who spent 24 years in the Marine Corps before retiring as a full colonel. "It's what they can do and what they have in their hearts and heads. Not what they looked like."

Hilgartner proudly says his battalion had no racial incidents while under his command.

So it was for Davis, 2nd Platoon and the many other courageous Marines of Bravo Company as they dug in and bravely fought a determined enemy in the Que Son Valley during Operation Swift. MacNichol, who is white, has long maintained that he has never experienced such a deep, binding camaraderie – either before or since - as that shared by the outnumbered Marines in that valley.

"It was a real special time, the first time in my life where all I cared about were the guys around me – black or white," he said. "We were all Americans just trying to stay alive."

In fact, Posey said he had no recollections of any such conversations with Davis or anyone else for that matter about any of the many tumultuous happenings back in the States, including the ongoing African-American fight for equality.

"I think we just had enough to do, day-to-day things," he said. "I can't remember even thinking about it."

Because none of that mattered along the frontlines of Vietnam.

It never occurred to Davis at that critical moment on Sept. 6, 1967 that the five men nearest him in the trench – Posey, Brackeen, Leedom, Hinshaw and Crandall – were all white.

They were *ALL* his brothers, and Davis was no stranger to looking out after his own.

"We can think and speculate on the race question forever," Posey said, "but it's not hard to sit here 42 years later and try to understand what happened and why. The answer stares us in the face. Rodney didn't stop to think about race. It didn't mean anything to him. He reacted instantly with overwhelming courage. That courage awes and humbles me to this day.

"I think that's the real lesson here. That is what I prefer to gain from the experience."

CHAPTER 14

WHAT HIS LEGACY MEANS TODAY

"A nation reveals itself by the men it produces, but also by the men it honors, the men it remembers."

President John F. Kennedy

Davis' has been gone now for 50 years, yet his enduring legacy remains strong. It shines brightest in the form of his family, most notably his two daughters, his four surviving siblings, three grandsons and an array of nieces, nephews and countless other family and friends who will always cherish his memory.

Gordon Davis has often said that he still deeply believes in his heart that his brother somehow thought he'd be OK even if he jumped on the grenade to save his buddies, that nothing bad could ever happen to him because he was a Marine.

In a sense, he was right.

The legacy of Sgt. Rodney M. Davis will easily outlast all those who knew him personally, making him larger in death than most likely ever possible in life. His body may no longer be with us, but his indomitable spirit and inspirational story continue to touch people from all over the world while making a positive difference in their lives.

Though tragically cut short, Davis' life continues to inspire his surviving family to action, namely in the form of the annual Davis

Family Reunions, the volunteer work done on his behalf and in the nearby housing complex named in his honor for those in need.

As Macon's only Medal of Honor recipient, he continues to be feted as such in a city and state steeped in an abiding pride of its long and distinguished military tradition. All of Macon and folks from around the country all took notice on November 10, 2012 when the Sgt. Rodney M. Davis Memorial Statue was formally unveiled on the 237th anniversary of the U.S. Marine Corps, as well as the announcement of the creation of the Sgt. Rodney M. Davis Memorial Scholarship. Always gung-ho and refusing to ever take no for an answer, Lt. Nicholas Warr, a former Marine platoon commander in Vietnam, headed a devoted group of retired 1/5 Marines who overcame a sluggish economy to raise roughly $80,000 in just six months to honor one of their own and make the memorable event possible.

Local and national media outlets – including cable giant CNN - had gathered in force as several of the men who survived that awful Sept. 6, 1967 day in the Que Son Valley and their families had made their way to Macon to celebrate the honor with a proud Davis family as part of the nation's many Veteran's Day festivities that weekend.

Roughly 500 people, including many elected state and local officials, were on hand at Linwood Cemetery for the moving tribute.

Added honors soon followed in a heartfelt letter dated Nov. 16, 2012 from U.S. Senator Johnny Isakson (R-Ga.) that echoed thoughts already shared by many of those who personally knew Sgt. Davis.

"To Members of the Davis Family:

It is an honor to convey to you my sincere appreciation for the loyal and dedicated service of Sergeant Rodney M. Davis during his time in the United States Marine Corps upon the dedication of his memorial statue. This fine and brave young man saved the lives of five of his fellow Marines without a thought to his own safety and paid the ultimate price. Sergeant Davis' service to our nation was exemplary, and I know the members of his family are proud that on Nov. 10, 2012, his love for his country and for his fellow Marines was recognized with the dedication of the Sergeant Rodney M. Davis

Memorial Monument, which will forever honor Macon's only Medal of Honor recipient. Without men like Sergeant Davis, the citizens of our great country would not enjoy the freedoms which so many take for granted.

I respect and admire our military personnel, and your beloved Rodney was the best of the best. He will live forever in your hearts, and this memorial monument will honor him and be a remembrance of this brave and loyal warrior who gave his life for his country.

With my warmest personal regards,

Sincerely,

Johnny Isakson"

That memorable accolade had come nearly a year after a collective effort by elected officials

A trace of Sgt. Rodney M. Davis' name on the Vietnam War Memorial in Washington, D.C.

statewide led to a dedication of a stretch of interstate highway in Macon to be named in Sgt. Rodney M. Davis' honor in November 2011.

It was the least the Macon community could do for "a true American hero" like Sgt. Rodney M. Davis, said Lt. Col. Michael Johnson, the commander at the time of the Marine detachment at nearby Robins Air Force Base.

"Individuals like Sgt. Davis are what make America great," he said.

A permanent exhibit at a city museum, a painting of Davis' likeness inside City Hall and picturesque statues of him placed in front of City Hall and at the nearby Macon Coliseum all testify to the great reverence in which his hometown and entire state of Georgia as a whole holds its heroes.

The spectre of Davis can likewise be readily found at the Pentagon, where the U.S. military honors Davis and all other Medal of Honor recipients in perpetuity with an inscription in its sacred "Hall of Heroes" in a special room at the Pentagon.

Davis was among the 18 inductees to the inaugural Georgia Military Veterans Hall of Fame on November 22, 2013 and among the state's 27 Medal of Honor recipients – including four living ones – recognized at a University of Georgia football game earlier that month.

He was one of Georgia's 12 Medal of Honor recipients from the Vietnam War to be feted under the gold dome of the state capitol in Atlanta on March 25, 2014. Gov. Nathan Deal and Major Gen. James E. Livingston (USMC, Ret.), himself a Medal of Honor recipient from the Vietnam War, were on hand to praise all Vietnam Veterans, but especially lauded Davis and the state's other Medal of Honor recipients who displayed gallantry above and beyond the call of duty in making the ultimate sacrifice on behalf of their country.

The recent spate of attention means that even many current active duty Marines too young to have even been alive at the time of his death have since come to know a little of Davis.

About how he lived as much as how he died.

It was for that very reason that more than 100 current and retired Marines put their own busy lives on hold to gather for the first time on one special Saturday on April 18, 2009 as they descended upon Macon from great distances in some cases to begin refurbishing their hero's gravesite. They were active duty and reservists; others retired, but forever Marines.

One such Marine, reservist Jason Greene of Atlanta, was not only a week shy of his own wedding at the time, but in the midst of closing on a house and preparing for his own upcoming deployment to Afghanistan. Yet, he was the one spearheading the charge on the daylong project.

The third-generation Marine said he felt obligated to do no less.

"There's an unspeakable feeling in my body about being a Marine, and about those who came before me," Greene, then 32, said. "I am indebted to this guy who made the ultimate sacrifice for his friends. It makes you wonder about it. I think of myself in that situation and wonder if I could do that for my Marines.

"I hope that I could be as courageous as Rodney was."

These dedicated Marines have returned to Macon twice a year since then, joining members of the Davis family and members of the community in making sure the gravesite of the city's greatest hero always remains presentable and worthy of such an icon.

Along the way, these duty-bound Marines have become considerably much more than that to the Davis family, each now proudly greeted as a beloved extended member of the family.

The Marines say they could have done no less.

"What all of the Marines of the gravesite detail are doing is living proof of 'Semper Fidelis,' " Posey said. "Always faithful and, I guarantee you, that's the way they all feel. Race means nothing in the Corps. We are Marines and [Sgt. Rodney M. Davis] was one of us. Nothing more, nothing less. Ask any Marine coming home from Afghanistan or Iraq, they will say the same."

Davis' lasting imprint can also be found many places elsewhere, well beyond the confined borders of Macon, Georgia. The USS Rodney M. Davis (FFG-60), the Oliver Hazard Perry class guided missile frigate named in his honor, proudly carried his name and inspirational story all over the world from 1987 to its recent decommissioning in 2015.

Powerfully displacing more than 4,100 tons of water at more than 453 feet long and 45 feet wide, the USS Rodney M. Davis was the Navy's first warship named after an African-American Medal of Honor recipient and just the fourth overall Navy vessel named after an African-American of any sort.

Aboard the Everett, Washington-based warship named in his honor, one could easily see the appropriately titled motto "By Valor and Arms" found on the ship's coat of arms. The dark blue and gold on the shield represent those colors traditionally associated with the Navy, according to the ship's website.

The shield also features "a heraldic grenade that represents the enemy grenade upon which Sgt. Rodney Maxwell Davis (USMC) threw himself when it landed in the midst of his platoon in Quang Nam Province, Republic of Vietnam, on 6 September, 1967." The grenade, with its chevrons representing sergeant's stripes, is shown placed on a pale suggesting containment, further symbolizing Davis' brave action which saved the lives of many of his fellow Marines and enabled the platoon to hold its ground, according to the ship's website.

The crest features a heraldic pelican, which is believed in antiquity to have wounded her breast with her own long, curved bill in order to draw blood for the purpose of feeding her young. It is said to be symbolic of Davis' selfless act by which he gave his own life to save others.

The light blue collar with a suspended gold inverted star alludes to the Medal of Honor awarded Davis, while the sprig of bamboo signifies South Vietnam, where he fought and died.

The late Lt. Gen. Frank E. Petersen (USMC, Ret.) was a veteran of both the Korean and Vietnam wars and was the Marine Corp's first African-American aviator and its first African-American general. He was the commanding general of the Marine Corps Combat Development Command when he gave the keynote address during the commissioning of the USS Rodney M. Davis in 1987.

He praised Davis' valor at that critical moment.

"We who are Marines hold such men in awe," Petersen said in his speech. "For those who would judge the United States Marine Corps by the actions of a few, I would have them look at Rodney M. Davis, who served so honorably with the greatest of sacrifice.

"I don't know how such men as Sgt. Davis can perform such acts of heroism, but I do know that I will never learn to bury such warriors. As we honor such men today, we do so humbly. They are truly America's heroes."

A replica of Davis' Marine dress blue uniform and accompanying medals and citations hung in the ship's mess decks for all hands to see. An accompanying display includes his Medal of Honor citation, medals, pictures and a photo of his name on the Vietnam War Memorial in Washington, D.C.

As of 2010, each new sailor – Black, White, Hispanic, Native-American or otherwise - coming aboard the USS Rodney M. Davis was required to first check in with then-Command Senior Chief Tracy Hunt, who was then the ship's highest-ranking enlisted man. He mandated they all quickly learn of the ship's history and of Sgt. Davis in particular.

Deployed under the operational control of U.S. Naval Forces Southern Command (NAVSO) as part of a Joint/Inter-Agency Task force conducting counter-narcotics trafficking operations in the Caribbean and Eastern Pacific, the USS Rodney M. Davis made sure to annually celebrate its namesake's birthday every April 7.

No matter where in the world the ship might have been at the time.

"The crew needs to understand and respect the namesake," said Commander Doug Stuffle, the ship's skipper from November 2008 through May 2010. "It's important. It brings camaraderie; it brings a sense of purpose that we're not just a ship out here doing something for nothing.

"It's important [crew members] understand. Their lives are what they are today because of sacrifices by people like Rodney M. Davis. So it's important for us to pay tribute and honor that."

Davis' rousing story resonated even closer to home for Stuffle, who overcame growing up in poverty to make something of himself.

"It tells you that greatness can come from anywhere," he said, "I'm a kid who grew up on welfare in Northern Idaho without any running water, and now I'm commanding a ship that was named because of [Davis'] action. I'm not saying I'm great by any means, but to be able to rise up and do something different from what people may have thought that you were destined to be. Same for him. He goes and, all of a sudden, he's famous, he wins the Medal of Honor and saves the lives of several or many Marines that were in his company.

"It's a fantastic story. It says a lot about the man. Every day, our sailors exemplify his characteristics of honor, courage and commitment. He's a shining example of that."

Hunt was still stationed in Williamsburg, Virginia in 2003 as part of a Navy Cargo Handling Battalion working in support of Operation Enduring Freedom in Iraq when he first read Davis' Medal of Honor citation and came away impressed.

"That's the one thing I take from all Medals of Honor [recipients]," he said, "they were thinking of others first. We can all apply more of that in our lives."

It was later that Hunt learned through a good friend then serving aboard the ship that Rodney M. Davis was an African-American like himself.

So he was especially thrilled to later learn in the summer of 2009 that he'd been assigned to the ship as its next Command Senior Chief.

"I called my Mom, my family and my friends!" Hunt recalled. "Some of them didn't know there are many African-Americans that received the Medal of Honor. Others need to know more about our American history and our heroes."

It was a powerful feeling shared by many whose lives were touched by Sgt. Rodney M. Davis long after his death in Vietnam, the ripples of his life still serving today like a stone skipping across a lake.

Brian Byrne, a retired sailor, was one such person who felt likewise when he announced on the social network Facebook on Veterans Day in November 2013 that he had named his new-born son Cannon Davis Byrne in honor of the man whose name graces the ship on which he had proudly served from 1999-2002.

The U.S. Navy announced plans in early 2014 to decommission its entire frigate fleet – including the USS Rodney M. Davis - by the end of the 2015. The warship honoring Macon's lone Medal of Honor recipient was decommissioned following its last day of active duty service in late March 2015 and will be sold to a yet-to-be-named friendly nation such as Australia, Taiwan, Turkey, Poland or Spain, according to Navy officials.

The formal decommissioning ceremony for the USS Rodney M. Davis took place at Naval Station Everett on Jan. 23, 2015.

****

The USS Rodney M. Davis (FFG-60) (photo courtesy of the U.S. Navy)

His life and death have come to mean different things to different people in the time that has since passed. All who shared a personal connection Davis still refer to him with a great reverence, each taking considerable pride in fondly recalling his memory and passing on their knowledge of for all he stood to upcoming generations.

His two daughters, Nicky and Samantha, are adults now, with Samantha and her husband now boasting three children of their own. Too young at the time he was killed to have remembered anything about their father, Nicky and Samantha have come to know him over the years by all they have read and been told by family and close friends.

People like their mother, Judy, before she succumbed to cancer in 2005. People like Granny. And people like their father's four siblings, all of whom still reside in Macon or in the surrounding area.

Rodney Davis will always be considerably more to his two daughters and surviving family than just one of the few African-Americans ever honored with the Medal of Honor. And a lot more than just another of the more than 58,000 names so powerfully inscribed on the Vietnam War Memorial in Washington, D.C. Rodney Davis' name can be found on Panel 26E, Line 8.

To his daughters, he will always be Dad, the tall and strikingly handsome Marine whose charms helped him immediately win over their mother's heart upon their first meeting in London, and keep it throughout the rest of her life. The same quiet, but firm man who took the greatest pleasure in spending his free time doting on his small children as much as possible before shipping out to Vietnam.

Nicky Davis was still a small, school-age child the first time she remembers being told by her mother her that her father was a hero.

Nicky didn't understand at the time just what exactly that meant, although she had already noticed by elementary school that she didn't have a father around like most of the rest of her classmates. She wasn't initially sure why that was the case, nor did she comprehend early on that her father had been killed while saving the lives of others.

It wasn't until a few years later when she was a teenager that Nicky began to completely grasp the gravity of what her father had done.

It was still tough news to take, and, though she has always been extremely proud, Nicky to this day rarely participates in any ceremonies honoring him.

"To me," Nicky Davis said, "it was always kind of bittersweet going to things like that. I would have gladly traded all of it to have my father."

As the offspring of a Medal of Honor recipient, both Nicky and Samantha had the option of attending their choice of any one of the nation's prestigious service academies in the U.S. Military Academy at West Point, the Naval Academy, the Air Force Academy or the Coast Guard Academy.

Neither daughter, however, chose to follow their father's footsteps into the military.

They instead preferred to join family members in collectively doing their best to make sure to always keep their father's memory alive. The Davis family honors him best daily by passing on all their considerable pride and what they knew of him, his values and his gallantry to their cadre of small children coming up behind them now.

Their efforts have already begun to take root as the family's next generation also learns about their heritage and assumes the mantle of extending that legacy.

Rodney M. Davis will always live through his family members as the proud Davis clan forever cherishes its own with its daily actions, as well as during its memorable annual family reunions and volunteer work done on his behalf.

Established in Rodney M. Davis' honor in the mid-1990s, the nearby Davis Family Homes offer affordable public housing for local Macon-area families in need. The Davis family felt this to be an appropriate gesture, lending a helping hand to those less capable of fending for themselves in much the same manner Rodney Davis had consistently done.

Ultimately at the expense of his own life.

His siblings still today experience the gamut of emotions when discussing their brother's untimely death, with equal amounts of great sadness in his loss and immeasurable pride in the way he deftly handled himself while saving the lives of his fellow Marines.

To them, he will forever be the loving brother who always had their backs. They knew him and loved him long before he became a Marine. Long before his valor at a critical moment in combat was later immortalized with the Medal of Honor, forever earning him a place in U.S. military lore.

He will always be just Rodney to them, a real person with real dreams, real personality and an unforgettable spirit about him.

"I want people to know what a warm and personable guy he was, always laughing and fiercely loyal and devoted," Gordon Davis said. "People always talk about him like he was this killing machine. But before he got to be the killing machine, he was a loving machine. He was really the most warm, personable person that you could have ever had the opportunity of knowing.

"I want people to know that."

****

That the five men closest to him at the battle's critical moment were all white and originally hailed from such distant places as Indiana, Iowa, Wisconsin, North Carolina and Texas respectively was of no consequence to Davis even as racial tensions boiled over back home thousands of miles away near the height of the Civil Rights Movement.

They were all Marines, eternal brothers-in-arms whose lives continued to feel Davis' presence many years later.

Now retired with the two adult children and two grandchildren he enjoys with his wife, Leedom still experiences nightmares regularly, often awaking to his own piercing screams in the middle of the night as his mind wanders back to that awful day and the heavy price Davis readily paid so that he might live.

For many years after their return home, he and Brackeen would always make sure to call one another every Sept. 6 to commemorate that unforgettable day just outside of Chau Lam.

They would often laugh, they would often cry. The two men would always remember their dear friends and fellow Marines who never came home. And how it was only possible they did so because of Sgt. Rodney M. Davis.

And what Leedom didn't personally know of Davis back then, he does now. He has not only made a point of getting to know all about the man who saved his own neck 50 years ago, but has made sure to also educate his family and the many others with whom he has come into contact over the years as well. Leedom speaks of Davis so frequently at home that he likes to joke that Kitty, his wife of more than 45 years, knows as much about the man who saved her husband's life as he does himself.

His two adult sons were still small children when he first began telling them of Sgt. Rodney M. Davis and how it was that his critical action on that memorable day in Vietnam paved the way for their very existence.

Leedom has visited the ship named in Davis' honor on several occasions, and even met his widow, the late Judy Davis, at a 1/5 reunion in the nation's capital in the 1993. It was Randy and Kitty Leedom's report following a stop in Macon at Davis' gravesite in August 2008 just after a 1/5 reunion in Jacksonville, Florida that quickly spurred the Marines back into action to clean up their hero's final resting site.

Leedom figured he owed Davis at least that much.

"The man saved my ass," Leedom said. "Sgt. Davis is my hero. He's my sons' heroes, too, because I tell 'em about that shit all the time. It's just something you don't ever forget. Thanks to Sgt. Davis, I'm still here."

Leedom was among the handful of retired 1/5 Marines in California for their 2009 Reunion who proudly accepted the invitation to come visit the current home of the First Battalion, Fifth Marines at Marine Corp Base, Camp Pendleton.

Surrounded at battalion headquarters by about a dozen active duty Marines, including several senior officers who had seen action in Afghanistan and Iraq, he immediately stopped in his tracks upon coming upon the framed picture of Sgt. Rodney M. Davis in the building's hallowed wing dedicated to 1/5 Medal of Honor recipients.

It suddenly became quiet enough to hear a pin drop as every Marine present was soon hanging on Leedom's every word as he recounted the events of that awful Sept. 6, 1967 day, and how he was forever indebted to Davis.

An emotional Leedom soon began sobbing uncontrollably and was unable to finish the story.

Petrous quickly picked up where his good friend could not and finished re-telling the powerful story of honor, courage and commitment as exemplified by Davis that fateful afternoon in the Que Son Valley.

"I've always thought about it," Petrous said. "I can't imagine anyone I have ever known making such a personal sacrifice. How much greater love can you have for your fellow Marines than to do that for guys you didn't even know that well?

"He was a true Marine."

Even now, Leedom wakes up every morning and commences his day by drinking his coffee from the specially-designed mug honoring Sgt. Rodney M. Davis. Leedom was in Macon in November 2012 when he met the Davis family for the first time and the sacrifice became real for both families. There was hardly a dry eye in the room.

Now a widower with two adult children, five grandchildren and three precious young great-grandchildren of his own, Posey initially struggled after returning from Vietnam, but later became a successful businessman after buying his wife's family company. Several family members accompanied him when he made his first trek to Macon to pay respects at Davis' gravesite in July 2009.

The two-time Purple Heart recipient wanted them to know all about the man who made their comfortable lives possible.

"I feel I owe it to him," an emotional Posey explained, referring to Davis. "Semper Fi, man."

Brackeen, who had six children and nine grandchildren at the time of his death in January 2010, penned a warmly received fictional novel, "A Night Drive" in 2009, recounting his experience in Operation Swift.

Brackeen never once discussed with his family what happened that fateful day just outside Chau Lam. But all of his children and even some of his grandchildren have since come away with at least a little understanding after reading his novel.

Some even more than most. Steven Brackeen Turunc, Brackeen's oldest grandson, created a memorial page on the social network Facebook in late September 2010 to honor his late grandfather. On another page, he paid tribute to Sgt. Rodney M. Davis, noting that it was only his sacrifice that allowed the entire Brackeen family to know his grandfather.

"He was a brave man and a good Marine," Steven Brackeen Turunc said of Davis in an e-mail from his home at the time in Paris. "My grandfather always told me that if [Davis] had not jumped on that grenade, every Marine in that trench would have been seriously injured or killed. My grandfather believed that he would have died that day. My mother would have been an orphan at the age of one, and I would have never known my grandfather. In a time when the United States was ravaged by racial tension, I wonder what kind of bond men form while fighting a war, for him to have saved the lives of a bunch of white men – including a Texan officer – that he knew for a short period of time?

"[Davis] was a modern-day hero, and the kind of Marine I strive to live up to."

Steven Brackeen Turunc arrived at Marine Corps Base Quantico in September 2014 to begin OCS and follow in his late grandfather's footsteps. Upon his graduation in late November, he received his commission as a Marine 2nd lieutenant.

Harold McConnell felt he could do no less from Tooele, Utah, the Salt Lake City suburb where he founded the Rodney M. Davis Marine Corps Detachment League. Created to preserve the traditions and promote the best interests of the Marine Corps, the league actively participates in the local community, raising funds for worthy causes and representing the Marine Corps at various functions.

McConnell had served on U.S. Embassy security detail in London alongside Davis for a little more than a year, and the two had developed a close friendship while living near one another in their comfortable barracks at St. John's Wood. They would often pal around together in their free time at the local pub across the street, where they would talk, laugh over drinks and "play darts with the blokes."

McConnell was eventually transferred in November 1965, just before the Corps began drawing Marines from out of even prestigious station posts from around the world like London and, instead, re-routing them to Vietnam. He remained unaware of Davis' death in Southeast Asia and the Medal of Honor-worthy circumstances until 2004.

Yet McConnell wasn't the least bit surprised when he finally did hear the news.

"He was just that type of guy," he said. "Rodney was that type of guy. He was there if you needed him."

Determined to honor his friend, McConnell formed the 40-man Rodney M. Davis Marine Corps Detachment League on August 9, 2006. It was he and other detachment members who later provided the USS Rodney M. Davis the exact replica of the namesake's Marine dress uniform and all the appropriate ribbons and citations. The League also put together a display of Davis' Medal of Honor citation, while also including a picture of his name on the Vietnam War Memorial in Washington, D.C. and additional photos of the ship's commissioning.

Semper Fidelis.

****

It's no small stretch to say that Rodney Davis could even be credited with possibly saving the lives of at least one of his brothers as well. Both Gordon Davis and Howard Davis would later voluntarily follow their brother's footsteps into the military, each serving as a military policeman with the U.S. Army. Howard Davis' unit had received its order to deploy to Vietnam in late 1971. Their plane had just touched down in Da Nang – the same airfield where Rodney Davis had first entered the country a little more than four years earlier – and the soldiers were eager to disembark. Weary from the long trip, Howard Davis and the rest of the soldiers with whom he had trained at Fort Polk in Louisiana quickly stood up and began filing out.

He had yet to step off the plane onto the tarmac when instructions came over the radio from higher-ups saying that Howard Davis was to instead stay aboard the plane and prepare to fly back to the U.S. Admittedly intent on going to Vietnam to exact revenge for the loss of his brother, Howard Davis was suddenly left confused and angry, resigned to remaining on that plane for eight hours before it would again lift off and take him back to the United States and out of harm's way.

Army officials informed him at the last minute that he would instead serve stateside rather than overseas. Howard Davis said he was later told that Army policy dictated that siblings of any family that had already lost a member to combat would not be sent to Vietnam. Some siblings still chose to go and fight even after the loss of a brother, but the Army was giving neither of the surviving Davis brothers such an option, according to Howard Davis.

Not when their brother was a Medal of Honor recipient who had already made the ultimate sacrifice on his country's behalf. The Davis family had suffered enough in proudly serving America.

Initially disappointed that he would not be able to join his close friends and fellow soldiers in Southeast Asia in the fight against communism on behalf of his late brother, Howard Davis soon came to realize that it was the right call for both him and his family.

He instead returned to the U.S. and honorably served at Fort Polk in Louisiana.

CHAPTER 15

CONCLUSION

Much has changed in the 50 years since Sgt. Rodney M. Davis gallantly joined the eternal pantheon of true American heroes.

Combat hot spots once long ago all-too-familiar to the general American public like Khe Sahn, Hue City, the Mekong Delta and the Que Son Valley have since been replaced with previously unknown locales like Fallujah, Kandahar, Marjah and Tora Bora as the United States has spent nearly all of this young century at war with radical murderous terrorists in both Iraq and Afghanistan. U.S. military forces have already largely left Iraq and have largely concluded major combat operations in Afghanistan as well.

But the same tireless dedication to duty and country that made heroes out of ordinary men like Sgt. Rodney M. Davis will always remain unchanged.

A new generation of champions has already begun to follow in his footsteps and those of the many others, often at risk to their own lives. Like their predecessors, honor, courage and commitment are a daily way of life rather than just mere empty words.

Rodney M. Davis was such a hero, one always proud to have been a part of something in the Marine Corps that was far bigger than himself.

Veterans will tell you that it is critically important that

upcoming generations know of stories like his because they need to always remember that freedom is never free, that it has instead always come with a steep price.

They say it's only in knowing of Davis and other heroes like him that today's young people can fully appreciate the special gift of liberty they've inherited and the tremendous amount of sacrifice required to keep it. The hope is that hearing such stories will inspire the next generation to become better citizens and somehow follow in the steps of greatness.

It didn't matter to Davis that the men closest to him in that trench were white, but it's easy now in hindsight to wonder whether it may have mattered at the time to those then back in his hometown wrestling with the heated issue of race. It appears that few people outside of Davis' unit – including those in his family - were ever aware that he willingly sacrificed his life for five fellow Marines, all of whom just happened to be white.

It makes you wonder whether such a revelation might have helped soothe Macon's tense racial environment at the time, even if just somewhat.

Macon, Georgia remains a largely segregated town even today, but it's not unreasonable to suggest that Davis' heroism in Vietnam still helped foster at least some racial healing in his own hometown. Race relations in the city have come a long way in the 50 years since his death, with his life and death coming in many ways to embody the meshing of the city's controversial past with its more promising future.

Rodney Davis' name is well-known throughout Macon these days, his heroism and deep love of country hailed by the city's black and white citizens alike. It's been amazing watching a city that once struggled with the issue of race come together in unison for the common purpose of honoring its most distinguished hero.

One who just happened to be African-American.

A statue of Davis now sits across from City Hall, located at the intersection of Monument and Poplar Streets and just a stone's throw from the much older busts from 1872 that celebrate the past accomplishments of Confederate men and women. Erected in the mid-1990s, the statue of Davis describes his valor in stone on one side, while the other depicts a U.S. Marine in combat.

The monument makes no mention of Davis' race.

"We can no longer call Rodney just our kin," his older brother Gordon has publicly stated.

"Rodney belongs to Macon and the world."